Praise for *Great Demo!*

"Anyone who has had to demonstrate software knows that a successful demo requires careful planning and execution. **Great Demo!** *is a straightforward, easy-to-read, and practical book that will guide you through this process. You often have only one chance to show your software. Peter Cohan uses his years of experience to help you make the most out of every opportunity."*

—Emanuel Rosen, author of *The Anatomy of Buzz* and former V.P.
Marketing, Niles Software

*"***Great Demo!** *not only shows you how to develop a great software demonstration, it also provides lots of food for thought for anyone demonstrating a product or trying to make a sale. This book full of real-world, practical suggestions and step-by-step ideas."*

—Gary Hoover, Founder, Hoover's, Inc.
(www.hoovers.com) and author, *Hoover's Vision*

"In **Great Demo!** Peter Cohan demonstrates the ultimate great demo, he writes a clear, focused book. Even more valuable than Peter's excellent grasp of his subject material is his ability to discuss it so practically. Simply stated, if you need to learn how to give a great software demo, look no further."

—Andrew J. Birol, Consultant, coach, speaker and author of *Focus. Accomplish. Grow.*

"If you've got an upcoming software demonstration to an important prospect, you've got two choices. You can fly by the seat of your pants, keep your fingers crossed and hope that you'll cross the finish line. Or you can read and apply what is in **Great Demo!** I've been involved giving or participating in software demos for 25 years. This is the best guide on the subject I've ever seen—by far."

—Dave Stein, author of *How Winners Sell*

GREAT DEMO!

Great Demo!

How To Create And Execute Stunning
Software Demonstrations

2nd Edition

Peter E. Cohan

iUniverse, Inc.
New York Lincoln Shanghai

Great Demo!
How To Create And Execute Stunning Software Demonstrations

Copyright © 2005 by Peter E. Cohan

iUniverse books may be ordered through booksellers or by contacting:

iUniverse
2021 Pine Lake Road, Suite 100
Lincoln, NE 68512
www.iuniverse.com
1-800-Authors (1-800-288-4677)

ISBN: 0-595-34559-X

Printed in the United States of America

It is better to ask some of the questions than to know all the answers.

—James Thurber, *Fables For Our Time & Famous Poems Illustrated* (1940) "The Scotty Who Knew Too Much"

Contents

About The Second Derivative

The Second Derivative was founded in 2003 to help organizations increase the probability of success in their sales and marketing processes. The Second Derivative provides a range of workshops, seminars, coaching, consulting, and skills development capabilities, with a particular focus on the needs of organizations developing and selling business-to-business software.

The Second Derivative helps organizations improve their marketing and sales results by providing novel methods for creating and delivering surprisingly compelling software demonstrations, resulting in rather dramatic increases in the rate of success. The Great Demo! method that is presented in this book is taught by The Second Derivative instructors to software businesses' pre-sales, sales, marketing and post-sales teams around the world.

The Second Derivative also offers and serves as the moderator for the DemoGurus community web-site (www.DemoGurus.com), where sales, pre-sales, and marketing people can go to get answers to questions on demos: Best practices, guidance on specific situations, tips, techniques, tools and the ability share ideas—to improve the effectiveness and ongoing success rate for their demonstrations. DemoGurus is an "evergreen" source for accessing and sharing information: "Great Stuff for Those Who Demo".

Current best practices, reviews of various tools, techniques, tips and a few fun items can be found on DemoGurus.

For more information on The Second Derivative, contact:

The Second Derivative

Website: www.SecondDerivative.com

Telephone: +1 (650) 631 3694

Email: PCohan@SecondDerivative.com

Mailing Address: 1538 Winding Way
                            Belmont, CA 94002

For more information on DemoGurus, contact:

DemoGurus

Website: www.DemoGurus.com

Telephone: +1 (650) 631 3694

Email: DemoGurus@SecondDerivative.com

Mailing Address: 1538 Winding Way
                            Belmont, CA 94002

To reach the Author, who welcomes your comments, suggestions, feedback and observations, please contact:

Peter Cohan

Website: www.SecondDerivative.com

Telephone: +1 (650) 631 3694

Email: PCohan@SecondDerivative.com

Mailing Address: 1538 Winding Way
                            Belmont, CA 94002

Introduction

These are exciting and challenging times in the software industry. It seems as though the Dot.com revolution was in another millennium (it was!), and software businesses are working harder than ever to realize their objectives. It is now more important than ever to connect and succeed in the sale and ongoing evolution of software tools.

You will find that this book shares experiences—both general and specific—gathered from years of customer interactions and hundreds (perhaps thousands!) of demonstrations.

Great Demo! provides guidelines and solutions for the three major challenges in constructing and presenting software demonstrations:

1. Customer qualification and needs analysis.
2. Organization of the content.
3. Infrastructure and technical issues.

While the primary beneficiaries are those in your organization who participate directly in the technical sales process, there are many job functions that will benefit through learning how to execute and deliver Great Demos.

Job titles and functions are often confusing, particularly between organizations. Salespeople are often called sales reps, account managers, or even sales consultants. The technical staff that supports the sales process often has a broader range of titles.

For the sake of clarity, this book uses the following terms:

Salesperson: I hope this one is easy! Other titles might include:

- Salesman or Saleswoman
- Sales Representative
- Account Manager
- Account Representative
- Sales Consultant

SE (Sales Engineer): This is the person who provides the technical expertise needed to complete the sale. He or she provides technical support for the sale of technology-based products. Other titles for the same role may include:

- Application Engineer
- Systems Engineer
- Technical Salesperson
- Sales Consultant
- Solution Architect
- Field Applications Scientist
- Technical Evangelist
- Implementation Specialist

Selling Team: This is the group of people that collectively are needed to complete the sale of a product to a customer. A Selling Team can be as small as a single Salesperson (not much of a team...) or include one or more of the following players:

- Salesperson
- Sales Engineer (SE)
- Consultant

- Development Staff
- Product Marketing staff
- Customer Support staff
- Senior Management
- Financial Staff

We'll use these definitions throughout this book. Additionally, a Glossary is included to act as a rapid reference while you read and to aid in refreshing your memory after you finish reading.

The book is loosely organized in the form of a Great Demo! Chapter 1 is an example of a Great Demo!, in written form. The next several chapters focus on understanding your own situation and on gaining an understanding of your customers' situations. These three chapters address qualification, research and preparation steps, similar to what you'd practice in a technical sales process.

Chapter 5 presents the Great Demo! strategy itself, followed by three key chapters on preparation. Chapters 9 and 10 are similar to a Question and Answer period in a demo, and provide tools for handling questions and special circumstances. Chapter 11 explores Remote Demonstrations, a topic that is growing in importance and interest, addressing issues and solutions for delivering demos over the web.

Finally, Chapters 12, 13 and 14 provide tools for the improving practitioner who wants to advance to higher levels of effectiveness.

Axioms, Anecdotes, Notes and *Exercises* are sprinkled throughout the book, to underscore key points, to offer examples, and to stimulate thought. I strongly recommend that you actually <u>do</u> the exercises! They are certainly not hard, but they will offer you enormous insight and pragmatic information for you to draw upon as you begin to prepare your own Great Demos.

A series of Appendixes is also included, offering examples of tools that you can apply right away.

I sincerely hope you find this manual useful and entertaining. Enjoy! I am confident that you will soon hear the following words from your Selling Team <u>and</u> your customers,

"... Wow, that was a Great Demo!"

1
What Is Great Demo?

The Answer

This is really simple and very powerful. Here's the answer: <u>Do The Last Thing First</u>.

That's right. Simply bring the end of your demo to the very front and you'll have a highly compelling, awesome, knock-their-socks-off demo.

Certainly there's more to this, but if you take nothing else away from this book, take this: <u>Do The Last Thing First</u>.

Remember the "7 Habits" book, by Steven Covey? Recall his "begin with the end in mind" concept? It is very similar to what I am proposing to you now. Most important, it works. It works great. It works so well that it may boggle your mind with how simple, how direct, and how obvious this was—once you've tried it and seen it work.

A Little More of the Answer

Certainly there's more to this, and now that I have your attention, I'll run through the concept rapidly, without much explanation, to give you the gist. Once we've completed this rapid overview, we can begin to explore the concept in as much detail as you like.

1. Begin your demo by showing the best, most compelling screen or handful of screens. You have to complete this in less than

two minutes—no longer. These screens <u>must</u> show your solution in the strongest possible form. You want your audience to be thinking "How did you do that?" Now you've got <u>their</u> attention!

2. Once your audience has grasped that a solution is possible, walk through how you get to those few screens. Do it smoothly, rapidly, confidently, but without any detailed explanation. Use only enough verbal comments to fill in while your software is operating. You need to finish this portion in less than four minutes—make it look fast and easy.

3. Now, if you are on target, your audience will ask you to show <u>how</u> you got to your concluding screens in more detail. They'll guide you to present and show the key capabilities they need and want. You can take as long as you need for this section, but typically you won't need more than 20 or 30 minutes.

You're done. You've closed them. They are convinced and ready to learn how they can bring your product aboard.

Now wasn't that easy?

Exercise: *Pick up this morning's newspaper and think about two things:*

1. *How you read it.*

2. *How it is written.*

If you are like most people, you scan the newspaper for articles that catch your interest. For many articles, you may only read the headline and move on rapidly—you're not interested in the topic. Other articles engage your attention sufficiently to review the first few paragraphs, after which you stop and move on. Some articles you read all the way through, because they address a topic of real interest for you.

Journalists fill their newspapers every day with a broad range of articles and features—and yet, only a fraction of the printed words are actually read by any one subscriber. Does that cause readers to drop their subscriptions? Typically not—readers don't expect (or want!) to read their entire daily newspaper top-to-bottom. Instead, they want a fast, easy method to access the specific information they want, be it sports, weather, international news or local events.

Newspapers organize the information they present in accord with their customers' interest at two levels. The top level is organized by section—Front Page, Business, Sports, etc., setting the context for all articles in these sections.

Each individual article is cleverly and clearly organized to enable readers to make rapid decisions about their depth of interest. The headline presents the topic—providing a binary opportunity for readers to pursue it further or move on. The first one or two paragraphs of the article summarize the story, concisely. Many readers are completely satisfied with this level of information and read no further, and return to scanning headlines.

The subsequent paragraphs explore the story in more detail, generally from a range of perspectives. These paragraphs often repeat the key points while providing additional depth and increased granularity. Readers who are truly interested in the topic are the typical consumers of this level of information.

Consider organizing your demonstrations like a newspaper article. The Great Demo! method uses these same ideas. Great Demos start by presenting a "headline" succinctly and rapidly to capture an audience's interest. Once "hooked", you then present the key capabilities using a minimum of mouse clicks—in a fashion very much similar to reading the first couple of paragraphs in a newspaper article. The audience just wants a summary at this point—not all of the details! Finally, for audiences that are really interested, you can then dig deeper and explore the breadth and depth of the relevant capabilities, just as a reader might pursue consuming the balance of a newspaper article.

Follow this advice and you'll enjoy an increase in your software subscribers!

The Rest Of The Answer

The balance of this book is designed to present the methods and explanations to provide you with the skills you need to research, create, and execute Great Demos.

- You'll start by developing why these skills are important—the impact on your organization and your own success.

- You will learn how to prepare by gathering the critical information you need (never demo without it!).

- You will crystallize what makes your software offerings unique and how best to present and represent the capabilities you offer.

- You'll learn how to organize and orchestrate demos.

- You will equip yourself with the tools to improve your interactions with your sales organization and others within your company.

- You'll see how to manage the different types of customers in any audience.

- You'll become a skilled, confident, practiced, sought-after Demo Master!

Read on....

What Is The Most Important Problem You Face Today?

If you are a technical resource for field sales, you may find yourself asking:

- How many demos do I need to do before we get the business?

- Am I showing the right stuff (the right capabilities)?

- Does my audience fidget and look distracted for the first 20 minutes of my demo?

- Do people leave before I'm through?

- Do they seem to ask too many questions—or no questions at all?

- How can I best prepare for a demo?

- How come I do all the hard work and the sales rep gets the commission?

If you are a sales rep, you may be asking:

- Why does it take so long to close the technical sale?

- Why do my field technical staff's demos seem boring—am I too familiar with the material?

- How can I get my technical staff to understand and communicate the key points that will complete the sale?

- Why am I missing quota?

- How can I make more money?

- How can I get the most out of my time with the field technical staff?

- "Man, if he blows this demo we'll never get another chance to make the sale…"

- Why does "Joe" do his own demos?

If you are a regional or national sales manager, you must be asking:

- How will we make our quota and operations expenses numbers?

- How will I do 20% more this year than I did last year, with the same resources?

- Why do the sales reps favor using one field technical person—while at the same time other field technical resources appear to be underutilized?

- Why do we spend so much time creating so many detailed, custom demos?

If you are a product or marketing manager, you should be asking:

- How do I get the field to sell "my" product?

- What are the best tools that I can provide to the field to help them make their numbers?

- How come the field always/never wants me to visit customers with them?

If you are a trainer, you often may ask:

- How do I provide a good overview of the product before launching into the details?

- How do I keep my audience's attention for the next 1/2/3 days of training?

If you are a developer, you may find yourself asking:

- How can I best show the neat stuff I've created?

- Demo? What do they want me to do?

- What the heck I am doing here?

If you are the CEO, COO, CFO, or CTO, you must be asking:

- What does it take to build a world-class sales engine?

- How can we increase our profitability using the existing organization?

- What do we need to do to improve the predictability of our sales forecast?

Exercise: *Take a piece of paper and write down your current quarter and full year's objectives, from memory. Compare these objectives with your current status. Are you in pain? (Or, are you in denial?)*

Successful demos may be the critical capability you need to address the challenges you face. A demonstration that goes well means sales, revenues, growth, and repeat business. A failed demo may mean the end of the world, as you know it!

2

Why Do Demos Fail?

What makes one demo a raging success and another a boring failure? Do you loathe watching demos? Do you hate doing demos?

Let's start by examining why many demonstrations fail. This may be cathartic for you; it will certainly be helpful to gain an understanding for the factors involved in giving demos.

Exercise: Grab a piece of paper and begin brainstorming: in your experience, what has happened at demos you've seen or given that caused them to fail or not succeed? List as many reasons as you can.

Now take a look at the following list of reasons for failed demonstrations—consolidated from the results of numerous workshops and hundreds (perhaps thousands!) of demos:

- A feature failed—software bugs or crashes
- Failure to identify the Critical Business Issues
- Demonstrator didn't know the product
- Unknown or unqualified audience needs
- Can't drive the message
- No story

- Confusing story
- Too long
- Too boring
- Too many features
- Didn't stop in time (demoed additional features that were not needed)
- Got lost in the story
- Unclear story
- No point to the story
- No conclusion or poor conclusion
- Broad range of audience needs
- Disconnect between the Salesperson and the Demonstrator
- Capabilities didn't match needs
- Lack of demo skills
- Lack of clear objectives for the demo
- Too little time
- Too much time
- Equipment failure
- Equipment unavailable
- Questions interrupted the flow
- People (coming/going) interrupted the flow

Clearly, there are many, many reasons why things can go wrong. How many of these have occurred during your demos? Which of these are the most important? Which can be controlled and which have direct impact on success?

When you examine these reasons closely you'll find that they tend to form three groups:

1. Technical or infrastructural problems.

2. Issues with the content and organization of the material.

3. Failure to qualify or adequately understand the customer's needs and interests.

We'll explore how to address each of these areas in the pages that follow—that's the objective of this book. Intrigued? Curious? Read on!

3

What Happens If The Demo Fails?

This chapter could well be entitled, "What <u>Bad Thing</u> Happens If The Demo Fails?" If the previous section gave you slight discomfort, this chapter will be certain to generate serious angst. And that is indeed the point. Let's understand how important a successful demo is to you and your organization—versus a failed demo.

Exercise: *What is the direct cost for a demo? That is, identify the cost of your time, your Salesperson's time, travel expenses and any other direct costs that are associated with giving a demo. List as many as you can and then calculate the sum of all of the costs.*

Exercise: *What is the full cost for the demo? What will it mean for your demo to be a success or a failure for you, your customer, and your company? List who is impacted and how they are impacted. Then take a deep breath…!*

Every year, software companies lose millions of dollars due to bad demos, poor demos, boring demos, misguided demos and misinformed demos. And most companies don't even know that the money is being lost!

The Origin Of Problem(s)

Demonstrations pervade many aspects of a software business—they are not just limited to sales processes. For example, in the development of new software, programmers often demonstrate new capabilities or implementations to their colleagues in marketing. This is, in fact, where many (most?) demo "pathways" originate—with the programmer.

They have created sufficient code to show off a new capability to their team members in marketing that follows a fairly narrow pathway, due to the immaturity of the code. When the marketing folks show the early versions of the product to customers, they typically follow that same pathway since they know it will (most likely) work properly and not run into any bugs or broken code. This cycle then continues as the product matures and the same demo pathways are shown over and over again.

Think about this for a moment. This means that many (most, again?) of your demonstrations come from developers—people who are not necessary known for being customer-focused!

Additionally, consider the evolution of a software product and its corresponding demonstrations. Version 1 is generally well-targeted and focused on specific customer problems—and the demonstrations created with Version 1 are similarly reasonably focused.

However, with Version 2 a series of new features and functions are added. Many of these are then added to the existing demonstrations to show off the new capabilities. The same thing happens with Version 3, 4, 5, and so on…

Have you ever seen a demo get shorter as the software matures? Very doubtful! We tend to show more and more capabilities as the product grows, forcing our audiences to watch and attempt to absorb more and more information with each release. Rather scary, when you think about it!

Exercise: Take a look at your "flagship" product. What is its current version?

Go back to the original demonstrations from earlier versions and compare with the current demos: are they longer? If so, by how much?

Your Sales Cup Is (At Least) Half Empty

Ask yourself: "How many technical visits and demonstrations does it take to close the sale?" If the answer is more than one demo to close any specific individual, then you are throwing away money, both in terms of operating costs and in the form of the most valuable resource of all: your time.

Let's examine the following possible sales process (you can work through your own in just a minute...):

> Let's say you have a booth at a trade show. Someone comes by the booth, sees some of the marketing materials describing your software and gets interested enough to want to learn more. He walks up to a demo station and asks for a demo. Your guy in the booth gives him the standard tradeshow demo. The customer watches and then asks for literature to be sent to him, then goes on to another booth.
>
> A few days after the trade show, the leads have been processed and passed to the sales reps, who begin calling and following-up. Your Salesperson calls the customer and does a terrific job in identifying the customer's situation, his critical business issues, and the specific capabilities he needs. The Salesperson is excited, because the customer has a key problem that your

tools can address very well and has budgeted to purchase a solution.

Your Salesperson asks if the customer has seen a demo at the tradeshow. He says yes, but he also volunteers that he didn't really see what he was looking for. The Salesperson convinces him that the tradeshow demo was not representative of the specific capabilities the customer wants, and the customer agrees to set up a meeting at his site to see another demo and discuss business terms. The meeting is set for later in the month.

The Salesperson coordinates internally and arranges for one of the field technical staff (let's give this person the generic title "Sales Engineer"—or SE for short) to join the Salesperson at the customer site for the meeting. Both fly to an airport near the customer, the morning of the demo, from different locations, and meet briefly before going in to see the customer. The SE is one of the most knowledgeable in the company regarding your software. He knows it inside and out. The Salesperson asks him to give a great demo, noting, "This guy is ready to buy". They are both confident since the SE has done dozens of demos.

The meeting starts and the customer has invited a few of his colleagues to join the meeting, mostly technical staff. The Salesperson outlines the interactions to date and then invites the SE to begin the demo. The SE does, what he feels, is a terrific job. He wants to make sure that they see all of the important capabilities. He carefully guides them through the software, building up a story that he has done numerous times before. Twenty minutes into the demo, the customer's technical staff are looking a bit bored, but politely continue to watch. They start to ask a few questions. The SE feels he knows his stuff and responds to the questions, and shows off the software accordingly, taking five minutes here, five minutes there for various questions. After an hour, he has completed the demo story and turns the meeting back to the Salesperson.

The original customer contact has been largely silent. He actually looks slightly disappointed and distracted. When your Salesperson starts to discuss business terms, including pricing, the customer listens briefly and then closes the meeting.

In the hallway on the way to the lobby, your Salesperson discusses "next steps" with the customer, but the customer is not interested in pursuing it further for the present. The Salesperson pursues this and asks, "Didn't you see what you need?"

The customer is frank and answers, candidly, "There seems to be a great deal of functionality in your product, but I felt I missed seeing what I was looking for—the specific capabilities I need." He is concerned that your product is too complex, that it will be too hard to use and too expensive to maintain. He admits that the key features he wants might be in the product, but he says he "kind of got lost" in the demo. Your Salesperson asks for one more chance and is able to convince the customer to agree, and they schedule another visit for the following week.

That evening, the Salesperson and the SE retreat to the bar of the hotel, and discuss the meeting. Both felt that they had showed the customer the key features of the product and didn't understand why he had missed them. The Salesperson really wants the business and together they build a plan to create a specific demo for the customer, based on the customer's data and work processes.

Once back in the office, the SE starts to work on the demo. He calls the technical staff he met at the customer and spends several hours discussing the customer's workflow and gathering detailed information. They send him some sample data and information on how they work. He then spends the next two days building a new, custom demo that uses the customer's data and integrates their workflow.

The day before the meeting, the Salesperson and the SE fly to the customer's city and meet in a hotel room to review the demo. They work hard, make some changes, refine, and develop what they feel is a knockout demo. They feel ready to go.

The next morning they drive to the customer's site and begin the meeting. The same people, for the most part, are present as at the last session. The Salesperson re-summarizes the key needs of the customer and the specific capabilities required to address those needs. The SE carefully and directly runs through the custom demo, clearly demonstrating and highlighting the specific capabilities.

The customer and his staff are now convinced—the technical sale has finally been completed, and the Salesperson works through pricing and payment terms. They get the order and all is well!

Or is it? Remember, these are top performers in your company. Why did it take two tries to get the order? What did this cost your company?

Let's examine what resources it took to close the technical sale. It required:

- One twenty-minute demo at the trade show.

- A two-person sales call (Salesperson and SE), including travel expenses.

- Two and one-half days of the SE's time preparing the demo.

- A second two-person sales call (Salesperson and SE), including travel expenses.

How much does that cost in your company? What other opportunities could you have pursued if your Salesperson and SE didn't have to make the second call, or both calls? What does this mean to your bottom line?

Here's how much this effort may have cost your company:

- Twenty minute demo: Didn't cost much in time, but your customer walked away unsatisfied and unfulfilled. No real damage, but no gain either. Hmmmm. Why even pay for the booth at the trade show if you aren't going to use it effectively?

  Cost: Booth construction, shipment, set-up, teardown, plus all of the travel and living costs (T & L) for the team at the tradeshow. Might as well save all of it, if you aren't going to make it pay. The cost for a booth and a team of people might range from a few thousand dollars to many tens of thousands of dollars.

- Your first two-person sales call: Now you are beginning to talk real cost both in time and opportunity. Figure $1,000 for each person for T&L, plus about $1,000 per person in salary and benefits per day. Total direct cost is $5,000 for this call. The opportunity cost is reflected in your now limited ability to meet with other customers—you can only be in front of one customer at a time, typically.

- SE preparation time: Two and a half days at $1,000 per day in salary and benefits is $2,500, plus again you are responsible for lost opportunities.

- Your second two-person sales call: Another $5,000, plus lost opportunities.

Total Investment:

- $12,500 in direct Salesperson and SE costs.

- $1,000's to $10,000's in trade-show costs, if you want to be cold and brutal about it.

- At least six and one half days worth of lost opportunities.

What about opportunity costs? These are very important on their own behalf. Consider the following:

> Typical Quota for a Salesperson: $2,000,000 per year

> Typical number of Selling-Days: 200 days per year

This means that your Salesperson must generate an average of $10,000 in sales for every selling-day. If the quota is $2,500,000 annually, then he or she must generate $12,500 for each selling-day. One way of quantifying opportunity cost is to use these numbers in addition to the direct costs calculated above.

Note: If this book can save you even one extra sales call, it was a terrific investment, wasn't it?!

But Wait, There's More

What is the real cost of a failed demo? It is, in fact, the sum of your company's direct costs, plus your customer's direct costs, plus all of the indirect, but very important costs. Let's explore.

Your company's direct costs, from above, may be on the order of $10,000.

Your customer's direct costs are also real, and need to be respected. After all, there is a real cost to your customer in bringing together the group of people for the meeting, as well as orchestrating that meeting.

For example, a one-hour meeting with 8 people may be $1,000 in direct costs. Two meetings, $2,000.

However, on the scale of things a few thousand dollars doesn't mean that much to you or your customer. Time does—time is something you can never get more of! People are jealous of their time, and if they think you've wasted their time you are not going to be in favor.

Further, what is the impact of a failed demo on you, on your sales team, product development, marketing, finance, administration…everyone, in fact, in your company? If you are a public company, what will it mean for your stock price?

A simple answer is that the impact of a failed demo is equal to the value of the sale, plus all potential future projects at that company. Think about the business you hope to do with any particular customer—how much is your typical software sale? What additional services are sold with the software: consulting services, installation services, implementation services, ongoing support, etc. What about future products, add-on modules and other new offerings?

All of these are at risk when a demo fails. The sum can be hundreds of thousands of dollars or even millions of dollars. Truly, the success or failure of your demo impacts the pending success of your entire company.

You Are The Point Of Focus

Consider the following: How long has it taken to develop products at your company? How many people have put countless hours into coding, QA, documentation, and configuration? Think about the effort invested in marketing, advertising, and finding customers. Remind yourself of all of the people in your firm and their roles in producing and supporting your products, and in running the business.

All of that effort, all of the hopes and expectations of everyone in your company will culminate in a 30 minute demo—<u>the</u> critical opportunity to make the connection between your company and your customer! <u>You</u> are the critical point of confluence between your entire organization and the users and supporters of your target customer. Think of it: You have the very few minutes of your demo to make the connection—and the business—happen! It looks like this:

Your Company (All at your company who make, sell, and support):			**Your Customer** (All at your customer who will benefit):
Sales	→		← Regular Users
Marketing	→		← Occasional Users
Support	→	YOU!	← Power Users
Development	→		← Support
Accounting	→		← Accounting
Management	→		← Management

You are the conduit of success—or failure. Frankly, you've got too many people counting on you to fail.

So, what if there is a way for you to be able to close the technical sale the first time? Let's focus on what you can do to substantially increase the probability of success.

4

Your Customer

Your Customer And Your Capabilities—Creating The Match

Now we are going to start building towards a solution. Your first steps are to begin to learn about your customer, and your customer's needs and challenges.

Exercise: Purchase and read a copy of "CustomerCentric Selling" or "Solution Selling: Creating Buyers in Difficult Selling Markets", listed in the Reading List Appendix. These are among the best manuals of operation for Salespeople and their teams.

Exercise: Even better, attend a "CustomerCentric Selling" or "Solution Selling" seminar. An interactive seminar is the best way to gain the information and insights from successful practitioners of skills.

Note: The Glossary contains brief, useful definitions of the key words and phrases used in this and the following chapters.

Target Your Audience

The first piece of information you need for your demo is to understand who is the target audience. Different titles and positions at your customer have different problems and needs. For the moment, put your own objectives and your products' capabilities behind you and focus on what your customer wants and needs.

Is this a demonstration for senior management? Or is it a demo for high-level technology leadership? Are you going to demo to technical staff? Operations people? IT people? Each group and each individual within the groups have their own specific issues and challenges.

Exercise: Consider: What is the biggest challenge you face in your job—that is, what is your most critical objective for the year?

Just as you have key objectives that you need to meet each quarter and each year, so do your customers. Each person typically has a different set of key objectives, dependent on his or her job and responsibilities. These key objectives are, rephrased, called Critical Business Issues (CBI's).

Let's use a simple example—a Salesperson in your company. What are the CBI's for a Salesperson? Typically a Salesperson has one CBI:

- Achieve or exceed quota.

As with all good objective-setting exercises, the more specific the more clear and powerful the message. For our Salesperson, you might re-state the CBI as:

- Achieve or exceed the quota of $____ in the Salesperson's region, for this quarter, selling currently available products.

That's clear—it has measurements of time and amount, with reasonable constraints. Now, if you ask this Salesperson how he or she is doing in the middle of the quarter in question, you will get one of two possible answers:

1. "I'm doing well—I expect to meet or exceed my quota—Yay!"

2. "I am unable to meet my quota—and this situation is not good!"

These two possible answers offer <u>very</u> powerful information. Michael Bosworth, in "Solution Selling", observes the following: "No Pain, No Change". Simple, but very powerful. If your Salesperson is already on track to meet or exceed quota then that Salesperson doesn't need any additional help—your Salesperson is not in "pain".

On the other hand, if your Salesperson is <u>not</u> on track to make quota, well, he or she is in a world of hurt! Serious pain! And since the Salesperson is in pain, he or she is very likely to be open to seeking solutions.

The next step is to understand <u>why</u> your Salesperson is not making quota: what are the <u>Reasons</u> for your Salesperson's inability to achieve quota? These Reasons are <u>very</u> important since each one represents an opportunity for a solution.

Let's explore.

Your Salesperson says, "I am concerned that I will be unable to achieve my quota this quarter."

You ask, "What do you think is causing this inability to achieve your quota? What are the reasons behind this problem?"

Salesperson says, "Well, I have done a great job qualifying prospects, and I've got lots of prospects, but we aren't completing the technical sale. Our demos are just not working. Our SE's don't seem to be able to connect with the audience and we are not showing the right stuff—the stuff our customers need. I spend days qualifying and preparing, but we don't seem to be able to close the technical sale. I don't understand it—I'm really frustrated." [Great example, huh?]

Let's summarize so far:

CBI: "Unable to achieve quota this quarter."

Reason: "Demonstrations are not working."

What's the solution? <u>What Specific Capabilities are needed to address this problem?</u>

Wow! Say that last sentence again, out loud. Do it! *"What Specific Capabilities Are Needed To Address This Problem?"* <u>Specific</u> Capabilities, not just <u>any</u> capabilities. Qualification skills aren't needed, and more prospects aren't needed.

The Specific Capabilities needed to address the Salesperson's Reason and solve the CBI are: <u>The specific skills and expertise to give Great Demos</u>. These skills must enable SE's to connect with their audience and to close the technical sale.

This is a terrifically important point that you must map to every demonstration situation: your customer is only truly interested in the Specific Capabilities needed to address his or her key problem. Anything else that you show may be interesting, possibly, but will only be distracting until you've demonstrated the Specific Capabilities needed. This is why many demos fail—the demo may never show the Specific Capabilities your customer wants. No wonder customers get bored, frustrated, or even hostile during some demos!

Anecdote: You are riding a bicycle rather fast. You skid on some gravel and fall, scrapping your legs and arms. You are bleeding moderately and you hurt, but your bike seems to be ok.

Someone sees you fall and comes to offer help. He offers you water—but you aren't thirsty, you're bleeding. He offers you a patch kit for your bike, but your tires are fine—and you are still bleeding. Now you are not only hurt, but also irritated! He offers food, music, asthma medicine, dancing girls, a new chain, handlebars, bicycle bags, a map, and a cell telephone.

All are very nice offers, but clearly what you need is:

1) a few bandages and

2) a couple of aspirin.

See how important <u>Specific</u> Capabilities are to providing a solution? See why customers get frustrated by general, untargeted demos?

The moral is clear: you need to demonstrate the Specific Capabilities needed to address the problem. You need to show the Specific Capabilities that address the Reason for the CBI.

Summarizing, each member of your audience has his or her own CBI's, Reasons, and the Specific Capabilities needed to address the Reasons. In the case of our Salesperson example, we find the following:

CBI:	"Unable to achieve quota this quarter."
Reason:	"Demonstrations are not working."
Specific Capabilities:	Demonstration Skills for the SE's involved, to enable them to present the Specific Capabilities needed by the customer to address the customer's CBI.

Exercise: Identify your three most typical job descriptions—that is, the people that you most often demonstrate to. Write down one CBI, one Reason, and one Specific Capability for each job description.

For extra credit, have four of your colleagues complete the same exercise—and compare and merge the answers.

The Chain of Pain

OK, now we understand how to identify one person's CBI, Reasons, and the Specific Capabilities needed to solve the CBI. What do you do when you have a group of people? After all, most demo situations aren't one-on-one, but rather involve a group as the audience. Is there any relationship between one person's CBI and another's?

Yes, indeed. Let's explore the following example, starting with the CEO of your organization. Let's assume that you work in a public company. That means, typically, that the most critical job for the CEO is to increase shareholder value:

CEO:

> CBI: Unable to increase shareholder value sufficiently, as measured by the stock price, on a quarter-by-quarter basis.

> Reason: Quarterly revenues, and hence profits, are less than expected by analysts.

VP Sales:

> CBI: Unable to achieve quarterly corporate revenue targets with existing product lines and sales staff.

> Reason: Salespeople, as a whole, are not achieving quarterly quotas.

Salesperson:

> CBI: Unable to achieve quarterly quotas on a regular basis.

Reason:	Product demonstrations fail to close the technical sale.

SE:

CBI:	Unable to produce demonstrations sufficient to close the technical sale in the timeframe required.
Reason:	Lack of demonstration skills and understanding of customer CBI's and Reasons.

Note how pain flows downhill, as does the pressure to perform! From this simple example, you can clearly see how the CEO's Reason is the same as the VP Sales CBI, and how the VP Sales Reason is the Salesperson's CBI, and so forth. Note also, that your boss' Reason is your CBI—logical, isn't it? After all, your boss sets your objectives based on what he or she needs to have accomplished in order to help complete his or her objectives.

So, what do you need to do to properly prepare for a demonstration? Do you start by reviewing all of the features and functions of your product? Nope! You need to understand the CBI's and Reasons of the members of the audience and identify the Specific Capabilities needed to address the Reasons. But, what specific capabilities does your software offer that map directly to the CBI and Reasons of the CEO, for example? It is quite likely that none are directly relevant. That's where the Chain of Pain becomes a powerful tool.

Your objective is to identify the Specific Capabilities that your product offers that will solve the CBI's of one or more of the members of the audience. Then, you use the links in the Chain of Pain to map your solution upwards to show how your product will positively impact the final decision makers.

Additionally, it is typical that the higher the job title that you are able to positively impact with your product's capabilities, then the higher the perceived value of your solution.

Axiom: *Pain flows downhill; gain flows uphill.*

Let's re-summarize, because these steps are very important:

Step 1:   We identified the CBI's and Reasons of the members of the audience.

Step 2:   We organized these CBI's and Reasons into a Chain of Pain in order to understand the relationships between audience members and their CBI's and Reasons.

Step 3:   We review the capabilities of our product and identify the Specific Capabilities needed and appropriate for addressable CBI's and Reasons.

Now we are ready to begin to build our demonstration. We now know exactly what Specific Capabilities to show. We also know which members of the audience will be receptive and interested, based on their CBI's and Reasons.

The Key Is Communication

About now you may be asking (especially if you are a SE), "Hey, am I in Sales or what?"

Good question. The fundamental issue behind that question is to understand who is responsible for unearthing the CBI's and Reasons of the customer. Functionally, this is the job of the Salesperson. Identification of CBI's, Reasons, and the development of the Chain of Pain is part of the qualification process that Salespeople typically practice.

For the present, let's assume that you have top-notch Salespeople in your organization, who are well skilled in identifying customer CBI's and Reasons. If this is the case, then your key to success is communication.

The simple requirement is for your Salesperson, sufficiently prior to the demonstration, to communicate to you the CBI's and Reasons uncovered during qualification. The truly tip-top Salesperson will also identify and communicate to you the Specific Capabilities needed for the demonstration.

If this process is not happening in your organization today, all you need to do to kick it off is to ask your Salespeople for that information. All you need to do is ask!

Exercise: Sit down with your favorite Salesperson and have him or her write down (use a whiteboard, for example) the CBI's, Reasons, and Specific Capabilities needed for the last major sale that took place. For extra credit, develop the customer's Chain of Pain as well.

This is a terrifically powerful exercise—by reviewing the CBI's, Reasons, Specific Capabilities and Chain of Pain for successful sales you are producing a "why did they buy" manual. This information is priceless!

What about situations where (God forbid) you are thrust into a demonstration situation without any prior knowledge of the customer's CBI's and Reasons? Is that possible? Could that happen? You <u>know</u> it will happen—for many SE's it has happened before, numerous times, and you should expect it to happen again!

The solution is simple. <u>You</u> need to invest a few minutes of the demonstration time to ask the questions and get the information you need.

"Hmmmm", I hear you say, "But I'm not trained for this!" This may seem a bit uncomfortable, asking questions about what people want or need. However, I can assure you that investing the energy and time to uncover a few CBI's and Reasons, and Specific Capabilities, if possible, will dramatically increase your probability of a successful demonstration session, and equally dramatically reduce the possibility of severe embarrassment due to a failed demo.

Simply stated, if you don't have the information you need, you should expect to fail. By gaining an understanding of your customer's CBI's, Reasons, and the Specific Capabilities, you are poised for success.

Exercise: Think about your own objectives and re-phrase them as CBI's. Consider—what bad thing(s) happens if you are unable to achieve your objectives and solve your CBI's? Write this down.

How does your inability to solve your CBI's impact others in your organization? Your peers, for example. Or your boss. Write down what bad thing happens to your boss if you are unable to solve your CBI's. Notice how the Chain of Pain works in both directions!

Now consider your customers. What bad thing(s) happens to them if they are unable to solve their CBI's?

Anecdote: You need to know what your customer needs. Pure and simple. This is the critical key to a successful demo. Let's explore this further: Try the following exercise the next time you are on an airplane. Let's assume that you have sat down next to someone, a stranger, and you engage in the standard conversation....

"Long day...."

"Yep. Just made the flight, too. Are you on business?"

"Yes, me too. What do you do?"

"I work for _____, and we _____...."

After a few minutes of conversation, you are both relaxed, sharing the kinship of fellow air travelers squashed into your seats. Now for the best part.

You ask, looking directly into your acquaintance's eyes:

"Tell me, what is the biggest challenge you face in your job today?"

The physical response is essentially always the same—and it is a physical response! Your seatmate pauses, focuses, takes a deep breath, and then…wham! Out comes his most important problem. The problem that keeps him awake at night and greets him in the shower in the morning—his Critical Business Issue. This is the problem that he must solve above all others, the problem that ultimately consumes his thoughts and actions.

Axiom: *There is an interesting relationship between the level of the job title and the ability of a person to clearly articulate their Critical Business Issues (CBI's) or objectives. Very simply, the higher one goes in an organization the higher the clarity.*

C-level staff and VP's can typically express their CBI's or objectives concisely and precisely. Directors and Managers are generally good at summarizing their CBI's and objectives, but will be less precise than their higher-level colleagues.

Other, more junior-level staff may actually find the question "What are your critical business issues or objectives?" hard to answer or even confusing!

The moral is to go higher in the organization if you want to gain more clarity with regards to individual and corporate needs.

Exercise: *Often, when you ask a customer, "What are your Critical Business Issues?" or "What are your objectives?" they may not be able to provide you with a good answer. This is sometimes because they haven't thought* about their day-to-day job in terms of their overall quarterly or annual objectives.

You can help get the information you need by guiding your customer with follow-on questions. For example, you can ask them about their quarterly or annual objectives and their status or progress against achieving them. This can help the customer think above and beyond their day-to-day tasks and chaos.

Using a very effective, but slightly different approach, you can ask, "How are you measured? In other words, at the end of the year, how do you know you deserve a raise? How do you determine whether you have been successful during the year?"

This last line of questioning often works very well for staff in more junior positions.

5

The Great Demo!

The Great Demo! Strategy

The Great Demo! strategy is very simple. It is the following pathway:

1. Present the Illustration—Summarize

2. Do It—Summarize

3. Do It Again—Summarize

4. Questions & Answers

5. Summarize

The essence of the Great Demo! strategy is in executing two things. First, show your audience the end of the demo right at the very beginning. The second key item is to focus and only show the Specific Capabilities needed to address the customer's problem.

This concept of turning the demo upside down may seem confusing, initially. After all, aren't we all expected to put together a "story", and follow that story through until we reach the end? And typically, the end shows the solution, the big "payoff" screen. It is what we've all been waiting for.

Consider this: why wait? Or more accurately, why force your customer to wait? Or worse, why force your customer to listen carefully, pay attention, and remember your example story for 20, 40, 60 minutes or more to finally get to the end—only to find that the end of the story is not what they have in mind?!

Exercise: Go to the local DMV or other complex government office (e.g., go get a new passport). Stand in the wrong line. How do you feel?

These are the two key reasons why many, perhaps most, demos fail. In the minds of the members of the audience…

1. "They never showed what I really needed to see."

2. "It took forever and I lost track."

Both outcomes are deadly. And expensive.

Give 'Em <u>What</u> They Need…

Great Demos focus on engaging the audience right from the beginning by showing them the Solution they need, right away. Once they have seen that what they need is a real possibility, they get interested very rapidly. Michael Bosworth calls this, generating "Hope and Curiosity." Seeing a Solution right away gives your customer the possibility, the <u>hope</u> that it might just work for them. And, it fills your audience with <u>curiosity</u>—they want to know <u>how</u> you can deliver that Solution. You'll find that your audience pursues <u>you</u> and drives your Great Demo! forward.

Another way of understanding this is to plan that you are going to show your audience a Solution in two ways. The first way is a very rapid description of <u>what</u> the Solution is. The second is a more thorough exploration of <u>how</u> that Solution works.

Exercise: Go shop for a new car. Initially, are you more interested in <u>what</u> the car looks like and the features it includes, or <u>how</u> to operate the car?

Once you see a car you like (the <u>what</u>), then do you want to learn about how the various controls work in more detail?

Exercise: How would you feel if you arrived at a new car dealership and a sales person grabbed you, whisked you into a car you didn't get a chance to look at, and then took you out on a test drive. Is your time being wasted?

Great Demos present the <u>what</u> right away, and then follow with the <u>how</u>.

...And <u>Only</u> What They Need

Great Demos focus on showing the audience <u>exactly</u> what they need—and leaving out everything else that might distract.

Exercise: Plan to go back to the car dealership, but before you leave, make a list of the car features that are most important to you.

When you arrive at the dealership, pretend that you have no idea what you want (…I know this is not honest, but this is an exercise, so please go with it…). Note what happens.

Most likely, the salesperson that meets you will ask a few questions, and then getting no real response, the salesperson will take you to see the most "popular" cars with the most "popular" features packages. Compare what the salesperson showed you against what you wrote down before you left.

Scary, isn't it?

The moral is to only show the Specific Capabilities your audience needs to solve their problem, their Critical Business Issue. While you <u>may</u> generate additional interest if you show other capabilities you run the huge risk of boring, alienating, or complicating your demo. You add risks:

- Risk of running into bugs or crashing.

- Risk of boring the audience.

- Risk of presenting capabilities that are not desired.

- Risk of running out of time <u>before</u> the audience has a chance to see what they need.

- Risk of confusing them with too many features and functions.

- Risk of making your product look too complicated.

- Risk of making your product look too expensive ("Why I am paying for all of these features I won't use?").

Anecdote: *True story: A salesperson had done an excellent job qualifying a customer, moving them through the sales process and had set up a final meeting to show the capabilities of the software. The Specific Capabilities were very clear—all the SE needed to do was to show those Specific Capabilities in a simple demo as the final step before completing the license agreement.*

The customer was ready to purchase 50 seats of the vendor's software, at an annual cost of ~$5,000 per seat—a $250,000 per year order. The audience included the lead customer player—the buyer—and a set of about a dozen end-users.

The SE, feeling that the customer would appreciate seeing more functionality and a richer breadth of the software, turned the demo into what he felt was an educational session. He showed lots of interesting (to the SE...)

capabilities and explained a broad range of functions. He turned a 10 minute demo into a 2-hour session.

At the end of the demo and the meeting, the customer buyer met with the balance of his team briefly, and then re-joined the salesperson for a wrap-up discussion.

The buyer told the salesperson that the software appeared much more com-plicated than they had originally expected. As a result, they had decided to purchase a <u>single</u> license and install it on a "power user's" machine. That power user would then service the other 49 users, who would bring their problems to the power user to work!

The result: The SE showed too many unnecessary features—making the software look too complex and confusing—which caused the customer to convert a 50 seat order into a 1 seat order. The demo <u>reduced</u> the value of the sale by $245,000 per year!

Now THAT is truly scary!

Make sure both the <u>what</u> and the <u>how</u> focus on the Specific Capabili-ties your customer needs. No more, no less.

Starting The Demo

Showing respect for your customer's time and needs is an important part of a Great Demo! I recommend beginning every demonstration with two questions:

1. What does your customer want to accomplish in the meet-ing—what are their objectives?

2. What are their time constraints?

Even if you already know your customer's objectives from pre-demon-stration discussions and communications, it is always intelligent to ask again. Why? First, it shows your genuine interest in mapping the time to what your customer wants to accomplish. Second, it is always possible that their needs or situation may have changed since your last communication.

Similarly, respecting your customer's time constraints is important. You may have previously agreed upon a certain amount of time for your meeting, confirming the time-constraints demonstrates professionalism. Again, it is possible that the situation has changed since the demonstration time was last confirmed—asking for your customer's time constraints allows any changes to be heard and addressed.

For example, you may find that the key person in the audience can only stay for the first 20 minutes of the meeting. You'll need to make sure that you prove your capabilities to this key person in that time or your whole effort may have been wasted.

Axiom: The most effective, important and influential people at any company are always in demand, and their time is limited.

The next three chapters on preparation will provide you with the tools and methods to help you create and deliver Great Demos.

You've just seen the <u>what</u>, now you'll learn the <u>how</u>!

6
Preparation

The key to <u>all</u> preparation for a Great Demo! is the identification of the Specific Capabilities needed to address your audience's Critical Business Issues (CBI's). Once these are clearly defined, your job is to map the capabilities of your software to show how they best provide those Specific Capabilities.

Now, where will this information come from? Whose responsibility is it to unearth a customer's CBI's, Reasons, and Specific Capabilities? How is this information translated into the components of a Great Demo?

What else is needed to properly prepare?

Exercise: Make a list of everything—hardware, software, equipment—that was missing or not working at demos you have seen or participated in during the past two years.

Axiom: Perspiration is inversely proportional to preparation.

Who is responsible for getting the hardware ready? Is the software up to date and working properly? What audio-visual equipment is needed? What about internet or network connections?

Preparation is a huge portion of the process of increasing the probability for success. Adequate preparation is a requirement for a Great Demo! Complete preparation increases your likelihood of success even further.

In the next two chapters we will examine the roles and relationship between the customer, the Salesperson and SE.

Important! *Whether you are in Sales or in a Technical role, you need to read* <u>*both*</u> *chapters. It is critical to understand one another's roles and to agree on the material and means of communication.*

For purposes of clarification, the "Sales" role includes anyone who is responsible for gathering and communicating CBI, Reason, and Specific Capabilities information coming from the customer into your organization. The "Technical" or SE role includes those people who are involved in creating the resulting demonstration and presenting it to the customer.

There may be one or more players involved with one or both roles. For example, a Salesperson may be a "professional" salesperson skilled at accessing and qualifying high-level job titles at customers, but that same Salesperson may be less knowledgeable about the specific technology issues and details that his software addresses. In this situation it may be incumbent on the SE to gather the lower-level, more detailed CBI, Reason, and Specific Capability information. In this case, both the Salesperson and SE participate in "Sales" roles.

In a second scenario, often found at new or younger companies, the Salesperson may both qualify customers and perform his or her own demonstrations. There may simply be no other technical resource available. In this case, the Salesperson is performing both roles.

7

Sales Preparation

The Role Of The Salesperson

The Salesperson has the ultimate responsibility to qualify a customer's needs. Specifically, the Salesperson must complete the following information in order to properly prepare for a Great Demo!:

1. Identify each member of the expected audience, their titles, and the relationships between the members of the audience.

2. For each member of the audience, identify that person's Critical Business Issues (CBI's), Reasons, and Specific Capabilities needed to solve each Reason and CBI.

3. Create the Chain of Pain for the audience members.

4. Determine the Objective for the demonstration meeting.

5. Set-up and define the meeting agenda and roles of the players—start and end times, introduction, demo, summary, etc.

6. Communicate all of the above information to the SE and other members of the Selling Team.

7. Reach agreement with the SE on which Specific Capabilities will be shown in the demonstration.

Clearly, item number 6 is hugely important! It is no help if all of the information on a customer's CBI's, Reasons, and Specific Capabilities is identified by the Salesperson but not communicated to the SE. This communication is absolutely critical—it is a crucial element for a Great Demo!

Exercise: *If you on the Sales side of things, when do you currently communicate account information to your Technical team member(s)?*

If you are in a Technical role, when do you most typically receive account information for an upcoming demo?

A highly typical response I often hear is, "In the car, in the parking lot, at the customer's site...!"

Let's examine each of these items further.

1. Identify Each Member of the Audience

This is simple and obvious; it is the first step in a qualification process. A key to increasing your likelihood for a successful demo is to truly understand the relationships between each member of the audience. It may also be helpful and important to include members of the customer who are not expected to be in attendance at the demo, but who nevertheless are important to the decision or implementation process. Frankly, the more you understand about your customer's people, organization, needs, and processes, the more likely it is that you will do business with that customer.

A tool that helps in communicating the audience titles and relationships is an organization chart. For example:

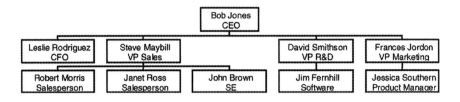

Most Salespeople use organization charts as standard practice. This first key to success is to share this information with the SE, and other members of the Selling Team, and to invest the time to discuss and understand all of the players and their relationships.

2. Identify Each Person's CBI's, Reasons, and Specific Capabilities

Next, use this organization chart as a template to fill out the CBI's, Reasons, and Specific Capabilities identified during qualification.

Qualification can be done by the Salesperson alone, if the Salesperson has a sufficient understanding of the capabilities of the products. This is, of course, the most efficient use of the Selling Team's (Salesperson and SE) time overall, since it requires only one person to handle the complete qualification task. Rejoice if your organization is rich in Salespeople who can qualify customers completely, including identifying the Specific Capabilities needed by each member of the customer.

Very often the Selling Team performs qualification as a team, with both the Salesperson and SE participating. Typically, the Salesperson asks the questions to help elucidate the customer's members, titles and responsibilities. The Salesperson should also identify the CBI's and Reasons. The SE is often needed to work with the Reasons to understand and identify the Specific Capabilities that are needed for each relevant member of the customer.

The Qualification process requires specific skills and expertise. It is central to the entire sales process and is important enough to invest in serious education for all members of the Selling Team. There are numerous books, seminars, and courses available that will provide the basic skills and processes—a few particularly good ones are identified in the Reading List Appendix. Once the basics are acquired, you need to practice, practice, practice!

Note: Michael Bosworth's books "CustomerCentric Selling" and "Solution Selling" provide exquisite information and processes to help you identify and detail a customer's CBI's, Reasons, and Specific Capabilities. The skills and methods described in "CustomerCentric Selling" and "Solution Selling" are particularly appropriate for high-value, intangible products such as many software offerings.

Note: An extremely effective method of elucidating a customer's CBI's, Reasons, and the Specific Capabilities needed is to have the customer map out their existing workflow. Mapping the current workflow enables you to ask questions about all of the customer members involved, their roles and responsibilities, and of course CBI's, Reasons, and Specific Capabilities.

The workflow map will also uncover the interdependencies between each member of the customer. These interdependencies are part of the basis for the Chain of Pain and can help increase the perceived value of your Solution, using your products and services.

Note: The power of the "Delta": The Delta is the difference between the way the customer does something today and the way it could be done using your Solution. This is a terrific way to understand and present value. A Delta can be in terms of time, people, steps, dollars, or any other measurable parameter that is important to the customer.

Often, it is easy to establish a Delta. For example:

Salesperson:	*"How long does it take for you to do this today?"*
Customer:	*"It takes three days with four people working on it full time."*
Salesperson:	*"What would you like this to be?"*
Customer:	*"We need to reduce this to one day, done by one person, to achieve our objectives this year." [BINGO! Your Delta is 11 person-days per cycle—there's your Reason for a CBI!]*

Now you know <u>both</u> what they need to accomplish <u>and</u> the direct value. In the simple example above, the direct value is the difference between three days with four people (12 person-days) versus one day with one person (1 person-day); the direct value is 11 person-days.

Later, you may also want to calculate the indirect value of this reduction of time and people for the customer. For example, what other activities or opportunities could be addressed with the additional 11 person-days—what is that value? What impact does this increased speed have on other members of the customer, on other processes?

Exercise: Map out <u>your</u> workflow—the workflow you currently use to target, find, qualify, sell, and implement your software with your customers. Include both the major steps and the people involved at each step.

For extra credit, identify the CBI's for each person involved.

Axiom: The Delta can be reduced to one of four possible measures:

1. *Cheaper.*
2. *Better.*

3. *Faster.*

4. *Couldn't Be Done Before.*

Work to understand and quantify the Delta in one or more of these terms.

Note: *Here is a truly terrific question to ask in a Qualification session: "Is there anything I should be asking that I haven't yet asked?"*

This is best done at the end of a discussion or Qualification session. It has the wonderful effect of causing your customer to pause and think, critically. Often your customer will come up with something that is important, which you both missed previously in your discussion.

Try it!

Once you (or the Selling Team as a whole) have identified the CBI's, Reasons, and Specific Capabilities needed, these all need to be added to your map of the organization. One simple way to accomplish this is to use the organization chart already created in Step 1, adding CBI, Reason and Specific Capability information for each person. I'll present this example in outline format:

CEO:

CBI:	Unable to increase shareholder value sufficiently, as measured by the stock price, on a quarter-by-quarter basis.
Reason:	Quarterly revenues, and hence profits, are less than expected by analysts.

CFO:

CBI:	Unable to achieve needed quarterly profits while working within existing budget.
Reason:	Marketing and sales costs per sale are unacceptably high.

Vice President R&D:

> CBI: Unable to deliver new product releases on time and on budget.

> Reason: Developers are not working on creating high-value new functionality.

Developer:

> CBI: Unable to create new functionality to meet critical customer needs.

> Reason: Unclear prioritization across a range of new potential features.

> Specific Capability Needed:

>> 1. Clear definition and prioritization of functions, features and new capabilities from Product Marketing.

VP Marketing:

> CBI: Unable to meet quarterly revenue targets with current marketing and advertising budget.

> Reason: Marketing unclear on why customers purchase specific products, making promotions and advertising ineffective.

Product Manager:

> CBI: Unable to achieve quarterly revenues for new products.

> Reason: Salespeople preferentially selling old products, as Salespeople are comfortable with old product's features and benefits statements.

> Specific Capabilities Needed:

>> 1. Elucidation and communication, to the Salespeople and SE's, of the CBI's, Reasons, and Specific Capabilities of customers that cannot be met by old products.
>> 2. Generation of Great Demos that enable Salespeople to close Projects (deals) with the new products rapidly.

VP Sales:

> CBI: Unable to achieve quarterly corporate revenue targets with existing product lines and sales staff.

Reason: Salespeople, as a whole, are not achieving quarterly quotas.

Salesperson:

CBI: Unable to achieve quarterly quotas on a regular basis.

Reason: Product demonstrations fail to close the technical sale.

Specific Capabilities Needed:

1. Great Demo! skills and methods for the SE's involved with each Project.
2. Elucidation and communication, to the SE's, of the CBI's, Reasons, and Specific Capabilities of the customer.

SE's:

CBI: Unable to produce demonstrations sufficient to close the technical sale in the time-frame required.

Reason: Lack of demonstration skills and understanding of customer CBI's and Reasons.

Specific Capabilities Needed:

1. Great Demo! skills and methods.
2. Clear communication of the Specific Capabilities needed to be demonstrated in the upcoming demo.

Your map of CBI's, Reasons, and Specific Capabilities is sufficiently complete for this example to proceed with creating your demonstration. The Specific Capabilities that can be addressed, in this example, by Great Demos are underlined in the example above.

There are many ways to lay out the customer's organization and to label CBI's, Reasons, and Specific Capabilities. The example above is a simple outline format. A Demonstration Information Worksheet is provided in the Appendix to help you gather and communicate this information in practice.

3. Identify the Chain Of Pain

The Chain of Pain illustrates the interdependencies between members of the organization. In the example above, you can see how everyone is impacted by the inability to deliver demonstrations that close the technical sale.

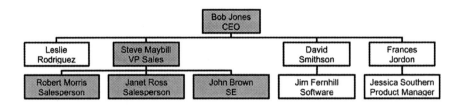

The gray boxes above show one Chain of Pain, from CEO, to VP Sales, to Salespeople, and finally to the SE's. A second Chain of Pain, again in grey, shows the connection between SE's, Software Developer, VP R&D, and the CEO.

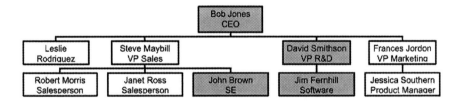

You can use the Chain of Pain to increase the perceived value of your Solution. In the example above, you can use the Delta technique to quantify the value of your solution for each person. For example, if the Developer is directed to work on the wrong capabilities for six months, due to poor identification and communication of the real capabilities needed, then that time may be completely wasted. If the cost of a fully burdened Developer is $250,000 per year, then the potential value of the skills presented in Great Demo! could be $125,000 for the Developer alone, not including the value of lost opportunities. Additionally, it is emotionally damaging for a Developer to work for a half a year creating an exquisite set of features that will never be used.

Exercise: *If this book saves your organization $125,000, please send me the difference between the $125,000 and the price of this book!*

---

4. Determine The Objective Of The Demonstration

What is it that you, the Selling Team, need to accomplish in this meeting? For many situations, your objective is to complete the technical sale. In other words, your objective is to show proof of the Specific Capabilities your Selling Team has represented to the customer.

You've identified their CBI's, their Reasons, and the Specific Capabilities they need. Budget is available and the timing is right. Your Selling Team has told the customer that your product will provide the Specific Capabilities desired. Now, the customer needs proof.

The objective is clear: you need to show the set of Specific Capabilities agreed upon to complete the project—that is the definition of closing the technical sale. Your demo must show those Specific Capabilities clearly and crisply.

Axiom: *Show only what is specifically needed—hold back on anything else. What if you have many other features and functions that would be cool to show? Don't do it. Hold them back. Focus on the proof at hand.*

Are there any other possible objectives for a demo? Certainly! Here are three general potential objectives for a demonstration:

- Technical Proof

- Vision Generation

- Information

We've just explored completing the Technical Sale by offering Technical Proof. A second possible objective is to create or generate a vision, for the customer, of what a Solution might look like.

Vision Generation is often a key part of the sales process. Generating a vision means to help a customer think in terms of solving their CBI's by using your products or services, through consuming the Specific Capabilities your customer needs.

Often, the process of Vision Generation and subsequently providing Technical Proof are separate steps in time. Sometimes, the same capabilities demonstrated for Vision Generation may become the Specific Capabilities demonstrated, again, in a Technical Proof session. Most often, capabilities or Specific Capabilities demonstrated in a Vision Generation demo are less detailed or less complete than in a Technical Proof session. Additionally, it is likely that Vision Generation is done with an initial set of customer members and Technical Proof is provided for a different, although often overlapping set.

Informational demonstrations are sometimes necessary, but are clearly risky! An informational demo may be requested at a trade show, or via a web site, or similar relatively unqualified route. The risk is simple: you may have no idea of the CBI's, Reasons, and Specific Capabilities needed by the customer and therefore risk presenting features and capabilities that have no value to the customer.

The moral is clear: avoid purely "informational" demos if at all possible. Invest in properly qualifying your customer and your reward will be more sales at lower cost. I'll provide additional methods to increase your probability of success for trade show demos and similar situations in Chapter 10, Special Situations.

Based on the concept of qualifying your customer before you demonstrate your software, we can redefine the types of demonstrations that you might do:

- Technical Proof
- Vision Generation
- ~~Information~~

Avoid doing "Information" demos! You should have a clear understanding of your objective and work a focused plan to achieve it.

5. Define The Meeting Agenda And Roles

It is the Salesperson's responsibility to define the meeting agenda, with the customer, and identify the roles and actions of the members of the Selling Team for the meeting. Specifically, the Salesperson needs to map out the following:

1. Meeting Location
2. Meeting Date
3. Meeting Start and End Times
4. Meeting Objective
5. Specific Roles and Timing
6. Customer Contact
7. Other Notes

This information needs to be agreed upon between the Selling Team and the customer, and additionally within the Selling Team. It is important to be consistent! Here is an example <u>Meeting Information Sheet</u> as an illustration:

Meeting Information Sheet

Meeting Location:	ABC Software Corporation 333 3rd Avenue Centerville, AZ 12345
Meeting Date:	Monday October 24, 2005.
Meeting Start Time:	9:00 AM
Meeting Ends:	10:30 AM
Meeting Objective:	Demonstrate Specific Capabilities agreed upon as Solution

Specific Roles/Timing:

9:00 AM	Introduction—Steve Maybill
9:10 AM	Review of Objectives, Reasons, and Specific Capabilities to Demonstrated—Salesperson
9:30 AM	Demonstration—SE
10:00 AM	Q&A—SE
10:10 AM	Summary—SE
10:20 AM	Next Steps and Wrap-Up—Salesperson
10:30 AM	Meeting Concludes

Customer Contact:

Steve Maybill, VP Sales

Telephone: +1 (555) 555 1212

Email: Smaybill@ABCSoftCorp.com

Other Notes: Meet Steve Maybill in Lobby of Building 1 at 8:50 AM

Blank and example Meeting Information Sheets are provided in the Appendix for your use.

6. Communicate Information To Full Selling Team

It is possible, or even likely, that the entire five steps above have been accomplished by a lone Salesperson, without the assistance of the SE or any other members of the Selling Team. Full qualification of the customer is, in fact, the first responsibility of the Salesperson. The next responsibility is the accurate communication of all of the proceeding information to the balance of the Selling Team, and especially to the SE responsible for creating and delivering the demonstration.

What needs to be communicated? All of the information gathered and organized in the previous five steps must be provided, and explained for clarity as necessary. The Salesperson <u>Demonstration Information Sheet</u> shown below and provided in the Appendix is an example of one format for ensuring that the full suite of information is successfully communicated.

Specifically, the Salesperson needs to provide the following items to the rest of the Selling Team, sufficiently prior to the demonstration date to give enough time to prepare:

1. Customer's organization chart and Chain(s) of Pain.

2. Meeting Objective.

3. Customer's key members and audience members' CBI's, Reasons, and Specific Capabilities needed to solve each Reason and CBI.

4. Meeting Agenda and Roles (Meeting Information Sheet).

Here is an example Demonstration Information Sheet:

Demonstration Information Sheet

Customer: ABC Software, Inc.

Meeting Date: October 24, 2005 at 9:00 AM

Customer Organization Charts and Chain(s) of Pain:

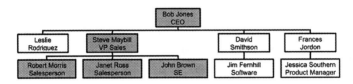

Meeting   Technical Proof.
Objective:

Customer CBI's, Reasons, and Specific Capabilities:

CEO:

    CBI: Unable to increase shareholder value sufficiently, as
                measured by the stock price, on a quarter-by-quarter basis.

    Reason: Quarterly revenues, and hence profits, are less than
                expected by analysts.

VP Sales:

    CBI: Unable to achieve quarterly corporate revenue targets with
                existing product lines and sales staff.

    Reason: Salespeople, as a whole, are not achieving quarterly quotas.

Salesperson:

    CBI: Unable to achieve quarterly quotas on a regular basis.

    Reason: Product demonstrations fail to close the technical sale.

    Specific Capabilities Needed:

        1. <u>Great Demo! skills and methods for the SE in the Project</u>.

        2. <u>Elucidation and communication, to the SE, of the CBI's,
        Reasons, and Specific capabilities of the customer</u>.

SE:

CBI:	Unable to produce demonstrations sufficient to close the technical sale in the time-frame required.
Reason:	Lack of demonstration skills and understanding of customer CBI's and Reasons.

Specific Capabilities Needed:

3. Great Demo! skills and methods.

4. Clear communication of the Specific Capabilities needed to be demonstrated in the upcoming Demo.

Meeting Information Sheet: (Attached)

Exercise: *What bad things happen if any of the information above is missing? Explore and write down an answer for each item. What would be the worst situation that could happen?*

Answer: Doing everything right but miscommunicating or lacking the identification of the Specific Capabilities needed. Nothing is worse than that!

---

7. Agree Upon Which Specific Capabilities Will Be Demonstrated

Let's assume that our Salesperson has done a superlative job with the previous six steps. All of the necessary information has been gathered and accurately communicated. Everyone knows what is needed for the demonstration meeting.

But—what if all of the Specific Capabilities are not available or cannot be demonstrated in the meeting?

Axiom: *No surprises, thank you very much!*

There could be many reasons for this. The product offerings could have changed. The product is at Alpha or Beta levels, and certain capabilities cannot be shown. There might be a bug that compromises demonstrating a certain capability. Whatever the reason, it is crucial that the Salesperson is aware and understands clearly which Specific Capabilities can be demonstrated, and which cannot.

The final step for the Salesperson is to reach agreement with the SE on which Specific Capabilities <u>will</u> be demonstrated and which will <u>not</u> be demonstrated. The Salesperson uses this information to prepare the introduction and summary for the meeting, overall.

Now all of the information necessary to create a Great Demo! is available and has been communicated to all members of the Selling Team. It's time for the SE to create the demo.

8
Technical Preparation

The Role Of The SE

The SE has the responsibility to translate the information provided in the Qualification and objective definition processes into a demonstration that achieves the objectives for the meeting. Specifically, the SE must create and be prepared to execute a demo that presents the Specific Capabilities in a logical manner and in context with the customer's situation. This combination of context and Specific Capabilities represents or directly demonstrates a Solution for the customer's Critical Business Issues (CBI's).

Axiom: A Solution is only a Solution if the customer agrees. In other words, a collection of Specific Capabilities is only a Solution if the customer sees how they solve the customer's CBI's.

Since you now have a complete list of the Specific Capabilities needed by the customer, you shouldn't choose to simply walk through the list, showing each one in order. This might be adequate, but it certainly won't be a Great Demo!

Your task is to translate the list of Specific Capabilities into a demonstration that presents these Specific Capabilities to the customer in the most logical, relevant and compelling pathway possible. The eleven steps to accomplish this are as follows:

1. Execute Research.

2. Coordinate Infrastructure with customer.

3. Create your Outline.

4. Create your Summary and Introduction.

5. Create your Illustration.

6. Develop the first pass (the "Do It").

7. Develop the second pass (the "Do It Again").

8. Practice.

9. Present to the Selling Team.

10. Adjust and Refine.

11. Confirm infrastructure with customer

Let's examine each of these items further.

1. Execute Research

Axiom: *Context is critical.*

Presenting a list of Specific Capabilities without reference to a customer's specific situation can result in a misaligned demonstration. While your probability of success will certainly be higher than presenting an unqualified set of features, you will substantially increase the likelihood of achieving the objective for the demonstration—showing a Solution—by understanding and presenting your list of Specific Capabilities in a context that is relevant for the customer.

For example, you may have a software product that provides the ability to create shapes with colors and tones of colors across the entire spectrum—this may in fact be <u>the</u> Specific Capability needed by the customer. However, if you present bright shades of orange, green and purple, you may be disappointed to find that the customer is really interested only in a variety of subtle flesh tones. Right Specific Capability, wrong context.

What can you do to gain an understanding of the customer's context? Ask a few questions; do some research.

The specific work you do will be largely dependent on the nature of your product offerings and capabilities, and the range of customer situations that you might encounter. The more vertical your offering, the more consolidated you might expect your customer situations to be. On the other hand, the more general your software is, the more important context becomes.

Exercise: List as many different customers and customer contexts as you can in 10 minutes for users of Microsoft PowerPoint.

Exercise: List as many customers and customer contexts as you can in 10 minutes for ChemDraw (an organic chemistry drawing program).

Exercise: List as many customers and customer contexts as you can in 10 minutes for one of your software products.

There are two types of research you can do:

1. Direct Research.

2. Indirect Research.

Direct Research is very simple: you contact your customer and ask questions. Your objective is to gain a clear understanding of example applications, problems, and desired solutions. Much of this information may have been elucidated during the Qualification process. Any missing information can be gathered by contacting the appropriate customer audience members and asking questions.

Where to begin? Start with the Meeting Information Sheet and call or email your key Customer Contact or Champion (a Champion is a customer representative who willingly and actively supports the purchase and implementation of your capabilities). Explain that you need to gather information that will help make the demonstration as useful and relevant as possible. Ask if the Customer Contact can provide you with the desired information, or, if not, if he or she will provide you with the names and contact information for others in the audience who do have the information.

You can also use the Organization Chart, from the Demonstration Information Sheet, as a source for additional contacts. Typically, before making contact, you will want to confirm with the Salesperson who you can contact freely and learn whether there are any special sensitivities or political issues to be aware of.

What information do you need? Your objective is to gather information that provides context, relevancy, and examples. The exact information you need is dependent on your product, the market, that customer, and many other factors. However, there are several standard pieces of information that can provide you with what you need:

- The Customer's Workflow. You can glean this from the Salesperson's (or your) notes taken during Qualification. Or, if the information is lacking, you can ask your customer contacts to outline their workflow for you. The workflow provides a logical sequence of events that your demonstration can follow.

- Example reports or documents. Often, the objective of a software product is to create a report or document faster, better, or cheaper than the current mechanism. Getting your hands on a few real examples is a terrific way to prepare. This provides you with examples of what your Illustration may want to look like.

- Specific Problems. Customers love to present challenges and see them solved. Asking your customer contacts to provide you with real problems that are typical of their situation gives you an accurate template both for the problem and the resolution. If you also ask how the solution needs to look (e.g. as a spreadsheet, document, presentation, etc.) and can see an example from the customer, then you have gathered excellent information. Once again, this information gives you a clear picture of what your Illustration should look like. <u>Warning! Make sure that the problem is tractable!</u> You need to ensure that the problem(s) your customer has so graciously provided are indeed solvable before agreeing to attempt them in a demo.

In all three cases above, you will want to agree with the customer that you <u>can and will</u> use their information in the demonstration. Getting this agreement is important—you don't want to compromise your customer contact(s) who may have thought they were only providing information as a template, and weren't expecting to see their specific data or examples shown for the entire audience.

Let's explore workflows a bit further. If your products or solutions impact a customer's workflow, you have a truly terrific opportunity to gather a rich set of extremely valuable information. This information helps both in the process of putting together and delivering your demonstrations, and in the overall sales process.

The best possible situation for exploring your customer's workflow is when you are in a face-to-face discussion, with a whiteboard or flipchart available. You can ask questions and begin to map out their workflow on the board. It is even better if you can hand your customer the pen and have them draw and present, while you take notes and ask questions.

Here's a simple process and examples of the kind of information you can learn:

- First, ask your customer to map out their current process. With a little guidance from you, they will provide you with information on:

  - Areas that are working poorly, including current bottlenecks and problem areas they want to address.

  - What is currently working fine today and does not need to be changed.

  - The people (names, relationships) involved in the workflow.

  - The time required for each step.

  - Other players and processes that may be impacted. ("Our workflow needs to speed up because we are the slow step in the overall processes in our company!")

  - Your exploration of their workflow will also provide with rich contextual information, including specific vocabulary and acronyms that your customer may use.

  - You should also learn how the output of the workflow is reported—this is critical information that will help you in preparing your Illustrations later in this chapter. Get examples of these reports, documents, forms, etc., if you are able to. At minimum, make sure to see examples so that you have a first-hand understanding of what they look like.

- Next, have your customer present their vision for a Solution, if they have one in mind. For example, they may say, "Well, we need to cut out this second step—it is taking way too long! We need the following capabilities to accomplish this…" Or you might hear, "We need to find a way eliminate this step because the department is losing two people…" It is possible that their level of vision development is rather thin—they may only know that changes are needed in order to meet their overall objectives. In the portion of the discussion, you can learn about:

  - Specific changes required to individual steps or the overall process. These can include steps to be eliminated, modified, added or integrated with other steps. It is likely you'll also uncover their desired Specific Capabilities in this discussion, if they don't call them out up-front or are unable to articulate them initially.

  - You can explore what changes might be needed regarding the output of the workflow—need sections to be added to reports, new alerts, "dashboards", and similar requirements. Again, this information will be extremely valuable to you in creating your Illustrations later on.

  - A <u>very</u> important set of information that you <u>need</u> to uncover is metrics on the time, people, or dollar savings needed by the customer to achieve their objectives. You can guide your customer through this process:

    You might ask, "How long does your process take today?"

    "It takes us 2 weeks and consumes 4 people during the entire time."

You can then ask, "What do you <u>need</u> this to become in order for you to achieve your objectives or your desired improvement?"

They might answer, "Well, we really need to get this down to 2 people over 2 days. And, we run this workflow about 20 times per year!"

The change between their current situation and their desired Solution provides you with the value of the Solution, based on <u>their</u> numbers (not based on the price of your software!).

In this example, the direct value of the Solution is 40 person-days (2 weeks of 5 working days times 4 people) minus 4 person-days (2 people over 2 days), times 20 cycles per year. The total direct value is therefore 36 x 20 person-days, which equals 720 person-days each year. That could turn out to be a substantial number!

This number is called the "Delta"—it is the value of a Solution based on the customer's data. You'll want capture this information in terms of a resource-based quantity: it needs to be based on money, time, or people.

Exercise: Using the example above, calculate the dollar value of this Solution if it was implemented at your company. Get your average FTE rate from your controller or accounting group (FTE rate, or "Full-Time-Equivalent rate, is the fully-loaded cost of an average employee—this includes salary, benefit, all relevant overhead, etc.). Next, ask them for the typical number of working days per year—this will generally be in the range 180-200. Then, plug that FTE rate into the equation to determine the dollar value.

For example, if your average FTE rate is $100,000 per year and the annual number of working days is 200, then the value of the Solution above will be (720/200) x $100,000 = $360,000 annually.

- When exploring the value through capturing the Delta of a Solution, there is an interesting but important subtlety that you may want to explore. This is the difference between what is <u>needed</u> by the customer to achieve their desired results or objectives, and what <u>additional gains</u> are possible. In the example above, you may be able to trim the customer's resource requirements in a Solution you propose even further—perhaps you can reduce the staff requirements to a single person performing the workflow in two days.

  While this may give you additional leverage, you should think carefully about how you choose to set expectations with your customer. I'd suggest erring on the conservative side of things, whenever possible.

  For example, you could say, "I believe that using the Specific Capabilities we provide, you can achieve your objective of reducing the cost and time of your work down to 2 people operating it during 2 days for each cycle. It <u>may</u> be possible to do even better than this, but that will depend of the specifics of your implementation."

- Finally, your exploration of your customer's workflow can also uncover opportunities for extending your current products to provide additional value. You may also find opportunities for completely new products or modules.

The process of Direct Research can offer an additional benefit for you: the creation of allies or supporters—or a real "Champion". The act of involving members of your customer's audience in the preparation process for a demonstration gives them a stake in the outcome. The more information from an audience member that is used, the higher will be their desire for their data and examples to look good.

For most technical or vertical market software products, one key success factor is cultivating and maintaining relationships with your customers. This needs to occur at all levels in your customer's organization. Your ability to establish good and growing relationships with the members of the audience, through Direct Research discussions, is a terrific beginning. By doing a good job in your demonstration, by using their information wisely and accurately, and by honoring the proprietary or confidential nature of the information they provide, you will earn their trust.

Anecdote: Hansruedi Kottmann, who has successfully sold and managed sales of scientific and technical software products for many, many years, calls this combination of trust and efficacy an <u>Earned Reputation</u>. Organizations, Salespeople, and SE's can all generate Earned Reputations.

Exercise: If you are a SE or Salesperson, sit down with your manager and define what specific steps you can take to generate an Earned Reputation for yourself. Set quarterly or annual objectives based on the steps necessary to achieve an Earned Reputation.

If you are a Sales Manager, Director, or Vice President of Sales or Services, gather your team and together define what specific steps you need to take to generate an Earned Reputation for your organization. Make these steps the basis for quarterly or annual objectives for your staff.

Exercise: Review the Exercise above and write CBI's, Reasons, and Specific Capabilities for yourself and your direct reporting chain. Identify and highlight the Chain of Pain in this organization structure.

Note: Confidentiality can be critical. Whenever you are receiving information from a customer that includes data, workflows, work processes, reports, documents or any other customer information, you must determine whether you need to put a Confidentiality or Non-Disclosure Agreement in place. These are legal documents that define what specifically will be treated as confidential information and the limitations on its use. Any information identified as confidential must be maintained as such—you cannot disclose it to any other organization or party.

If you have any questions regarding confidential information, Confidentiality or Non-Disclosure Agreements, definitely contact your legal department. You want to be absolutely clear before using the information you gather!

So, if you have been successful in gathering information for your demo via Direct Research, you may have a wonderful workflow, several excellent examples, and a spicy specific problem or two. You are ready to go on to the next step.

But wait! What if your customer is unwilling or unable to provide you with the information you seek? It is possible that the customer cannot provide specific examples, due to confidentiality, for example.

All is not lost; you can perform Indirect Research instead. Information gathered using Indirect Research is generally not as targeted, and hence is not as valuable, as information that you are able to get from Direct Research. Nevertheless, it is much better than nothing.

Exercise: *Go out to lunch or dinner with a colleague, your spouse or better half, or a friend. The more exotic the restaurant, the better. Order different items. Have your partner describe the flavors in their dishes to you. Try to imagine the taste. Now describe your dishes in return.*

Now, exchange your plates and taste one another's food.

How does the description you heard from your partner compare with your first-hand experience? This exercise improves with increasing number of people at the table, by the way. A few glasses of wine help as well...!

As with Direct Research, the information you need for your demo will be driven by the capabilities of your product(s), the market and the customer. Here are a number of sources for information that can be helpful:

- Customer's Web Site. So obvious! Web sites often provide excellent illustrations of customers' processes, workflows, and output. Tap into them...!. Additionally, since all of the information is in the public domain, there is no risk of compromising confidentiality.

- Papers, Reports, and Other Publications. If your product provides solutions for technical staff or scientists, the papers that the customer's staff publishes can provide wonderful material for your demo preparation. You can search public information sources, public and commercial databases, and conference proceedings for members of the customer's audience by name, by the company, or even topic.

  If you do choose to use information from customer publications, it is a good idea to contact the person or people whose data you plan to use and gain their permission or agreement before the demo takes place. Additionally, the act of contacting the person or people may provide the opportunity for you to gather Direct Research information, or at least to clarify any questions you might have regarding their publications. Often, people who might initially give you a chilly reception when you first request information can warm up considerably once they see you have "done your homework" to find information that they produced. You may actually create an ally!

- Patents. Patents can often provide rich sources of examples and information, but sometimes not, depending of the specific patent, its relationship with other patents, and your willingness to wade through them! In either case patents offer names or other specific terms that can be used in searches of other sources of information.

- Customer's Competition. It is likely that your customer's competitors are working on solving the same or very similar problems. Information gathered from one customer (public, not confidential information) may be relevant for another.

- Your Competition. Your competition may already have done your homework for you! Careful, here, however. Only use examples or information that you have gathered from your competition if

  - you are confident that your products offer significantly more or better implementation of the desired Specific Capabilities compared with your competitor's offering(s).

  - you are certain that they have read, understood, and are effectively utilizing this book.

OK. Now you have all the information you need, or are able to obtain, in order to prepare your demonstration. You are ready to start putting it together...or are you?

2. Coordinate Infrastructure With The Customer

Before you put together any pieces for your demo, make sure that you'll be able to show it!

Exercise: How many times have you gone to a conference, meeting, or similar event where the computer won't connect with an LCD projector, or the demonstration won't work because of the lack of an internet connection or other hardware?

When you are part of the audience, how do feel while you are waiting for the presenters to get their act together? Does it increase or decrease your estimation of their abilities and their products?

When you are part of the presenting team, how does it feel when you are struggling to get things connected and operating with the audience waiting, and growing more and more restless and hostile? Has this ever happened to you? Could it?

Preparation must include ensuring that the infrastructure required to show your demonstration will be in place and ready to go, at the time of your demo. It is your responsibility to make certain that everything you need is organized and ready.

An Infrastructure Checklist is a tool that can help you manage this. It is the list of all hardware, software, network, audio-visual, facilities and other requirements needed for your demonstration. Here are example requirements that could form your Infrastructure Checklist:

Hardware:

- Laptop Computer checked and operating correctly.
  - Sufficient space on hard disk.
  - RAM sufficient for application.

- Modem operating correctly.

- Screen resolution sufficient for application.

- Network or Server Computer checked and operating correctly (or Virtual Machine on your laptop).

  - Sufficient space on hard disk.

  - RAM sufficient for application.

  - Modem operating correctly.

  - Network connections ok.

- For Modem Connections:

  - Bring sufficient telephone cable to extend from computer to telephone jack.

  - Ascertain availability of an <u>analog</u> (or appropriate) telephone line in demonstration room.

  - Ensure that telephone line is connected and operating correctly.

  - Understand dialing requirements for line, e.g. "Dial 9 for an outside line".

- For Network Connections:

  - Bring sufficient network cable to extend from computer to network jack.

  - Ascertain availability of network connections in meeting room (physical or Wi-Fi).

  - Ensure that network is connected and operating correctly.

  - Understand any connection requirements.

- Projection (e.g., LCD Projector):

  - If it is your device, ensure that it is operating correctly and that your computer is compatible with the device.

  - Ensure that the device provides sufficient screen resolution to show your application well.

  - Ensure that it is available on the days and times required—you may need to reserve shared equipment in advance.

  - Make sure you understand how to operate it!

  - Make sure you know how (and when) to toggle your computer display between its own display and an external display.

  - If it is a rented device, confirm the top three previous items ahead of time, and pick up the device ahead of time to try it out and familiarize yourself with its controls. Make sure that any rented device is provided with instruction manuals or on-screen help.

  - If the device is the customer's, confirm the top three items ahead of time. Plan to schedule sufficient time after arriving but before the demo to test the device and familiarize yourself with it.

- Other Projection Equipment You May Need:

  - Overhead Projector.

  - RF Mouse.

  - Laser Pointer.

  - Videotape, VCR and TV Monitor.

  - CD-ROM or DVD drive.

- Power:

- Voltage/Current/Adapters—where is the demo taking place? U.S.? Europe? Japan? Antarctica? Make sure that you have the appropriate adapter plugs and voltage/current ratings for your equipment.

- Plugs—ensure that plugs are available and accessible where you need power.

- Extension Cord(s)—you may need one or more extension cords, depending on your situation. You may need to bring duct tape if you are going to run cords where people will walk, to tape cords down safely.

- Power Strip(s)—you may need one or more power strips, depending on the total number of plugs you need for your equipment.

- Lighting:

    - If you need a dimmed or darkened room for good viewing, confirm that the room indeed can be darkened. Are drapes or blinds available and do they work?

    - Make sure you understand how to operate the lights and room dimmers ahead of time. Many conference or presentation facilities offer extensive lighting controls, often from a podium control. Make sure you either understand how to operate these controls or ensure that someone who does is present.

- Screen(s):

    - Decide if you need one or more projection screens. You may choose to use an overhead projector, or one laptop, to show a Demo Roadmap (covered later in the book) on one screen and use a second screen for the actual demo.

    - Make sure that a screen is available if needed! You *can* project on a blank wall, but it isn't pleasant.

- Ensure that the screen size matches the room and audience sizes.

- Learn how to operate the motor controls for electric or
  automated screens.

- Audio:

  - Small rooms with small audiences (1-20 people) typically
    won't require sound reinforcement or microphones.

  - Large rooms may need microphones and speakers for you
    to be heard clearly. Make sure you learn how to operate
    the sound reinforcement controls to adjust the volume.

  - Make sure that you understand how to use remote or
    "clip-on" microphone(s), and how to adjust the sound
    level. Make sure that there are working and fresh batter-
    ies available!

- Whiteboard or Flipchart:

  - A whiteboard or flipchart may be essential for managing
    questions, creating a To Do List or Not Now List (pre-
    sented later in the book). Note that you can also create a
    Word document or two to accomplish the same tasks.

  - Similarly, having a whiteboard or flipchart available can
    be terrific for answering questions, drawing images,
    describing software architecture, etc.

  - Be sure to erase a customer's whiteboard and remove or
    trash flipchart pages before leaving the customer's site.

- Handouts and Props:

  Plan ahead and determine what handouts you need to bring
  and how many. You may also want to consider providing

certain handouts to a subset of your audience, according to need or interest. Handouts can include:

- Paper copies of your Illustration(s).
- Brochures, Fact Sheets, FAQ's.
- White Papers.
- Reference Stories.
- Corporate Folders and Backgrounders.
- CD-ROMs or DVDs.
- Give-aways.

Software:

- Laptop Computer software checked and operating correctly, including correct versions.
  - Windows (or Mac or Linux) operating system.
  - "Standard" software, e.g. MS Office.
  - Your product software.
  - Any ancillary products necessary for your product(s) to operate properly.
  - Any ancillary products that add value to your product(s) that you might want or need to use. Remember to consider software that may not be required for the demo, but may be necessary or helpful in answering questions.
- Network or Server Computer software checked and operating correctly.
  - Server software installation.
  - Network software installation.
  - Web server software.

- Database software, schema, tables.

An example Infrastructure Checklist is provided for your use in the Appendix. You are welcome to copy and edit it to meet your specific needs and situations. It can also be a terrific "welcome" gift for new SE's just joining your organization…!

Most of us take all of the above for granted—that the equipment we need will be available and operating. However, it is your responsibility to ensure that the demonstration goes smoothly. The lack of any critical piece of equipment could mean that all of your preparation work and time is wasted. You could even lose the sale if you don't get another chance to show your Specific Capabilities!

Make an Infrastructure Checklist for each demonstration. Divide it into two categories:

1. Required Items

2. Optional Items (that would be nice to have)

Make sure that all of your Required Items are ready for your demo and you'll have one less thing to worry about. You'll also have taken one more step to increase the probability of success and prepare the way for your Great Demo!

Why review your Infrastructure Checklist now, rather after your demo is all prepared? If any of your required items are not available or cannot be relied upon, then you will need to prepare your demonstration to work around these limitations.

For example, what if your desired demo would require an internet connection, but none will be available in the meeting room? Or, what if the new piece of software code you've been waiting for won't be ready in time (Gosh—could this ever happen?)? You'll need to build your demo to accommodate these restrictions (assuming that you can't change the venue or reschedule, in these two examples).

In any case, you must map your demonstration to the availability (or lack) of the infrastructure you need. An Example Infrastructure Checklist is included in the Appendix. You can copy and modify it for your own use.

Now, you have all the information you need to build your Great Demo! Let's get to work!

3. Create Your Outline

Your first step is to create your Outline. An Outline provides the structure for the general components of your demo. It defines the presence and order for the building blocks, or sections, of your demo, and includes general information for each section.

Axiom: *An Outline defines the "What", not the "How".*

Let's create a simple example: You've completed your research and have all the information you need from your Salesperson. In this simple case you are going to demo to one person who needs two Specific capabilities for his/her Solution. Both Specific Capabilities can be presented using one of your software products and both can be represented very well with a single Illustration.

While this may seem over simplified, the reality is that many Solutions require only two Specific Capabilities:

1. The ability to search for information and

2. The ability to report it in a manner that is acceptable and useful to the customer.

Often, a single Illustration that shows the report itself is sufficient (if not downright exciting!) to prove the Specific Capability. The reason for this is that in order to create the report, a search must have been performed.

Your demonstration Outline then consists of:

1. Introduction.

2. Present the Illustration (the completed report).

3. Rapidly create the query, perform the search, and present the report again. Follow with a brief summary.

4. Walk more deliberately through creating the query, performing the search, and creating and presenting the report, again. Summarize briefly.

5. Questions and Answers.

6. Final Summary.

For this simple demo, in the Introduction you describe these six steps. Your Outline is, in fact, your Introduction. You might say the following:

> "Thanks for inviting us here today. As Bob, our Salesperson said, I'm going to show you the ability to search and generate a report in the format you want, using your data. First, I'll show you the completed report itself. Next I'll show you rapidly how I prepared that report. I'll then run through that process again, in more detail. Finally, I'll summarize and then we can address any questions that are raised during this demo."

Notice that you literally restate the Specific Capabilities needed in your Introduction. You'll do the same thing each time you summarize. This will ensure that your audience truly understands that you have presented a Solution. It also will give the audience an opportunity to agree with the Solution, and accept it as a Solution. Remember that a Solution is <u>only</u> a Solution if the customer agrees that it will solve the CBI.

Terrific—now we have a good Outline for a simple case. But how do we handle situations that may have one or more CBI's that require multiple Solutions?

Demonstrations that show sets of Specific Capabilities necessary to support multiple Solutions are managed the same way as our simple example. Here's a general outline for a demo that requires two Solutions:

1. Introduction.

2. Present the Illustrations for <u>both</u> solutions.

3. Re-present the Illustration for the <u>first</u> Solution.

4. Rapidly demonstrate the <u>first</u> set of Specific Capabilities. Follow with a brief summary.

5. Walk more deliberately through demonstrating the <u>first</u> set of Specific Capabilities. Summarize for the <u>first</u> set of Specific Capabilities.

6. Introduce and present the Illustration for the <u>second</u> Solution.

7. Rapidly demonstrate the <u>second</u> set of Specific Capabilities. Follow with a brief summary.

8. Walk more deliberately through demonstrating the <u>second</u> set of Specific Capabilities. Summarize for the <u>second</u> set of Specific Capabilities.

9. Summarize for <u>both</u> sets of Specific Capabilities.

10. Questions and Answers.

11. Final summary.

What is particularly powerful about this guideline is that you are presenting <u>both</u> Illustrations right up front—showing the audience that there are indeed solutions to both CBI's very early in the demo.

For people who are interested solely in one solution, they are offered incentive to wait to see it in more detail, since you've revealed that a solution is indeed possible. You have set a hook…!

It may seem like you are summarizing a great deal in this example. In fact, you'll want to summarize at the end of each section to let people know that you've completed that section—this also provides an opportunity for your audience to agree with (or challenge) your Solution as presented. These frequent summaries also help to act as a road map, to let the audience know where they are in the demo.

The Summary in Step 9 is important and unique in that you are summarizing across all of the Specific Capabilities presented during the demo. You'll find, in fact, that a Summary and an Introduction are nearly the same, differing only in the dimension of time (this is not the Twilight Zone; the Intro information is presented at the beginning and the Summary information is presented at the end…).

So, now we have a formula for generating Outlines for your demonstrations:

1. Introduction.

2. Present the Illustrations for all of the Solutions.

3. For Each Solution,

    a. Re-present the Illustration for that Solution.

    b. Rapidly demonstrate that set of Specific Capabilities. Follow with a brief summary.

    c. Walk more deliberately through demonstrating that set of Specific Capabilities. Summarize for that set of Specific Capabilities.

4. Summarize for all sets of Specific Capabilities.

5. Questions and Answers.

6.   Final Summary.

Opportunity: *This is essentially a "Do-While" loop. Write a software program that will automatically generate a Great Demo! When you are finished, send it to me and we'll commercialize it.*

Guess what? All of the hard work is now done. All you need to do is to fill in the blanks!

4. Create Your Summary and Introduction

Why create your Summary before you create the rest of the demo? After all, doesn't the Summary come at the end?

Exercise: *Open your telephone directory to a random page. Find an address you don't recognize and have no idea where it is. Now get in your car and start driving, without consulting any maps. Let me know when you get there....!*

You need to know where you are going before you set out on a trip. Similarly, you need to know what you want to accomplish in your demonstration before you create your summary. Recall that you can have one or two Objectives for a demonstration:

- Technical Proof
- Vision Generation

You may choose to show the same capabilities, but your Summary needs to take into account whether the demo is to complete Technical Proof or Create a Vision.

In preparing for the demonstration we would review the Demonstration Information Sheet, provided by the Salesperson. We would then map the Objective into our Summary.

Let's go back to our simple example of a single Solution requiring two Specific Capabilities, a search and a report. Our Demonstration Information Sheet states that the Objective for the demo is Technical Proof. Here is an example Summary for this situation:

> "Thanks again for inviting us here today. In summary, let me review what we've completed this afternoon. Our objective was to prove our capabilities to you. I showed you the ability to search and generate a report in the format you want, using your data. Initially, I showed you the completed report itself. Then I showed you rapidly how I prepared that report. Next I then ran through that process again, in more detail. We then addressed the questions you raised regarding availability and support of our software.
>
> I believe that we met our objective this afternoon and that we do provide the ability to search and generate a report in the format you want, using your data. Thanks again for joining us this afternoon."

You could then close the meeting or turn it over to the Salesperson, according to the original plan in the Meeting Information Sheet.

Your formula for a Summary is to follow your Outline. You can build a Summary for a complex demo as follows:

1. "Thanks for inviting us. Our objective today was to…We shared a number of solutions with you. Let me review these in order.
   [Then, for each Solution,]

   a. I showed you the ability to [Specific Capability].

    b.   Initially, I showed you the [Illustration].

    c.   Then I showed you rapidly how I prepared that [Illustration].

    d.   I then ran through that process again, in more detail.

    e.   I believe that we showed that we do provide the ability to [Specific Capability].

2. We then addressed the questions raised during the demo. [Then, for each Question,]

    a.   Your question was [restate the question, briefly].

    b.   We said that [restate answer, briefly].

3. I believe that we met our objective this afternoon and that we do provide the abilities you need to address your problems. Thanks again for coming this afternoon."

And that's your Summary!

What about an Introduction? An Introduction contains the same form and elements as your Summary. The major difference is that you are describing what <u>will</u> happen in your Introduction, as opposed to what <u>did</u> happen in your Summary.

Your formula for an Introduction is to use your Summary, but to place the items in future tense. You can build an Introduction for a complex demo as follows:

1. "Thanks for inviting us. Out objective today is to…We will share a number of solutions with you.

2. First, I will briefly present an overview of each of the solutions I'll address [present each Illustration rapidly].

3. Next, I'll describe each solution in more detail.
   [Then, for each Solution,]

   a. I'll share with you the ability to [Specific Capability].

   b. Initially, I will show you an illustration.

   c. Then I'll show you, very rapidly, how to prepare that [Illustration].

   d. Then I'll run through that process again, in more detail.

4. We will then address any questions you raise during the demo.

5. Finally, I'll provide a summary of our time together and then turn the meeting back over to...."

Anecdote: Mrs. Sasuly, my 11th grade English teacher, told us, "Tell 'em what you are going to say, say it, and then tell 'em what you just told 'em."

Many others have offered the same advice, in sales training sessions, presentation skills courses, and in writing exercises. Nevertheless, as far as I was concerned, Mrs. Sasuly said it first and made it stick in my mind. Thanks, Mrs. Sasuly!

Now you have a Summary to end with and an Introduction to begin with. Let's get started with building your Illustration.

5. Create Your Illustration

OK, take a deep breath…This is it—the heart of the Great Demo! strategy: the Illustration.

Your Illustration is the single most important visual tool for your Great Demo! Humans are visual creatures. As audience members, we often hear but don't really listen to words coming from a Salesperson or the other members of a Selling Team. We do, however, evaluate images rapidly and carefully.

An Illustration is a concise, visual method of communicating the reality of a Solution. Often, an Illustration is a desired report, which may be generated from the results of a series of individual steps.

During your research steps, you will have identified key reports that either represent the customer's desired Solution or enable decisions that are the Solution. These reports can take numerous forms. They can be text documents, presentations, summaries, spreadsheets, web printouts, or collections of several individual components of these.

Your best Illustration will effectively mimic or form a report that includes the components and information desired. Your software products will either enable these reports to be created "cheaper-better-faster" or provide the ability to create reports that were previously not possible.

Axiom: *The best materials from which to create Illustrations are often found on the top of your customer's desks.*

Why? Because this is the most important work they need to complete. It will be on the top of their desks, often in the space they reserve for the current project—right in the middle.

When doing research, if possible, ask to visit your customer's office to talk or discuss details. If you are allowed, take a look at what is on their desk. You may well see the very report you want in progress!

Another likely location is on the customer's computer, in the "File 1-2-3-4" open menu. The files that your customer opens each morning and the applications that are launched every day often are the very reports, documents, dashboards, spreadsheets and portals that represent Illustrations for solutions they seek. Again, if you are able to ask for and receive examples or copies of these, then you are well on your way to creating highly compelling Illustrations.

A further location is your customer's office whiteboard. Many people keep track of their key projects or status using their whiteboard—this is often especially true for sales managers, who want to keep their key projects and major forecast components in their direct view. Your customer's whiteboard may offer you additional ideas for terrific Illustrations.

Finally, an additional logical place you might expect to find terrific examples of Illustrations is in your customer's briefcase or portfolio—quite often he or she will take current copies of these documents wherever they go.

Another strategy for creating your Illustration is to work directly with your customer to define what their desired report, output, or deliverable should look like. This is the most certain route, and offers you the additional advantage of guiding the contents of the report or deliverable such that it maps to the capabilities of your software products.

Anecdote: While working at a company that produced software for the chemical and pharmaceutical industry, we created a product that would bring together chemical structures with textual and numeric test results. A report that shows the relationship between various chemical structures and their impact on biological or other tests is called a "SAR Table". This is a standard report that is used throughout the chemical and pharmaceutical research community.

Prior to 1991, creating these reports involved a great deal of work, including an enormous amount of physical cutting and pasting, and copying of test and numeric information. You'd often find chemists desks with piles of printed structures and even larger piles of test results. Chemists literally spent hours every week working to integrate and correlate the correct structures with the correct test results.

Once they finally have a SAR Table report completed, they want to be able to make decisions based on the information. These decisions are critical in the process of discovering new drugs and materials. To make decisions, chemists need to be able to gather the information, correlate it, and then sort and search through the information according to specific parameters.

The company I worked for created a software product that would provide the ability to electronically search for desired structures and test data at one time (wow!) and to bring that resulting information into a table format for additional sorting, viewing, printing and discussion.

Determining the Illustration for this application was easy—it was a completed SAR Table itself.

Additionally, not only did chemists in industry have examples in process or completed on their desktops, but the SAR Table was a standard form for communicating Structure-Activity-Relationship information in industry journals. Finding examples that were relevant and on target was easy!

Should an Illustration be presented as an overhead, from printout, or as a live screen? This depends on what the preferred end product is. In other words, seek to understand both <u>what</u> the final product is and <u>how</u> it is consumed. Match your specific implementation of an Illustration to the manner in which it will be consumed by your customer.

Anecdote: *I saw an awesome Illustration presented using a "Blackberry" as the delivery vehicle. It was exactly appropriate for the situation and had the additional positive impact of being passed around the room from hand-to-hand. Truly remarkable!!*

Can more than one Illustration be appropriate for a particular Solution? Absolutely! You may, in fact, be required to show two or more Illustrations to prove the set of Specific Capabilities. Or, you may choose to build to a climax, by presenting a series of increasingly complex or complete Illustrations.

Anecdote: A particularly effective SE created three Illustrations for a particular Solution. The first Illustration was the baseline for what the customer needed. The second was an improved version, with more information presented in a clearer format. The third Illustration was designed to knock the customer's socks off—it showed everything the customer could have imagined.

This SE began his Introduction and then moved smoothly into presenting his Illustrations. He showed the first, which caused a number of people in the audience to ask, "How did you make that?"

He presented the second Illustration, and the audience response was even stronger. People literally were saying, "Please show us how you made those, now!"

When he presented the third Illustration, the audience literally went crazy. They had been working to create that same format report for years—and here it was right in front of their eyes. They <u>demanded</u> to learn how to generate that Illustration!

See how a strong Illustration drives a Great Demo? This demo was a huge success.

Presenting Illustrations

Your Illustrations may be the most important part of your demonstration. They generate "hope and curiosity". They present that fact that you <u>do</u> offer a Solution to a customer's CBI. Your Illustration is the first substantive thing your customer will see in your demo—you want to make the impact as strong and successful as possible.

To gain the greatest effect in presenting your Illustrations, execute the following process.

First, when you are preparing your demonstration and creating your Illustration(s), start by building a "Situation Slide". This slide will help to organize your thoughts and, more important, it will help the audience recall <u>their</u> situation.

If the Objective for your demonstration is Technical Proof, then creating the Situation Slide is easy—you are simply recalling what the customer has already told you about their situation.

Using PowerPoint (or similar tool), create a Situation Slide that contains the following information:

1. Customer: Company Name and Job Title of the key player (who "owns" the CBI).

2. CBI.

3. Reason(s).

4. Specific Capability(ies) needed.

5. The Delta (what is desired by the customer or what is possible using your Solution, or both, if possible).

Remember, you should express the Delta in terms of:

- Cheaper,

- Better,

- Faster, or

- Couldn't be done before.

The specific numbers in the Delta should be stated in terms of a resource:

- Money (Dollars, Euros, Yen, etc.),

- Time,

- People, or

- A combination.

The Delta is an expression of the value of your Solution in the customer's hands—this makes it especially important to include this information and draw attention to it.

The combination of a Situation Slide and associated Illustration(s) makes a concise, targeted presentation to a customer. Here's the process you should use in the demonstration meeting for a Technical Proof demo:

1. Present the Situation Slide. Simply review the information it contains and confirm with the customer that it is all correct. This re-establishes the situation for the customer and sets the scene.

2. Present the Illustration(s) for the Solution for that Situation. Follow these important steps:

   a. Describe what the audience is seeing in the Illustration(s). This only takes a few moments and it is highly effective in ensuring that your audience gains an understanding of the Illustration itself.

   b. Remind the audience of the Delta represented by the Solution. In particular, recall for them the <u>difference</u> between how the customer achieved their objective previously in comparison with how it is accomplished using your Solution.

Presenting your Situation Slide and Illustration in this manner sets up the balance of the demonstration beautifully. In many cases, when you present your Situation Slide and Illustration, members of your audience will actually say, "How did you do that?" They will naturally drive you to go into more detail—they have seen the "what" and want to learn about the "how"! You will satisfy their interest in the next sections, when you present the "Do It" and "Do It Again" pathways.

That's how to set-up and best present your Illustration for a Technical Proof demonstration. But what about a Vision Generation demonstration, where you may have little or no information regarding your customer's CBI's, Reasons, and desired Specific Capabilities?

You can use the same process, but with a simple (but important!) twist: Instead of creating a Situation Slide based on your customer's specific situation, you use a Situation Slide that represents an <u>expected</u> situation.

Determining what might be reasonable expected situations for a new customer is one of the key sales and marketing objectives. In a vertical market, you can generally expect that the CBI's, Reasons and Specific Capabilities for a job title at one company should be the same or similar for that same job title at another company. Therefore, if you have had success with one company with a specific Situation (job title, CBI, Reason(s), Specific Capabilities and Delta), you should have a reasonable probability of success in presenting that same (sanitized!) Situation and Illustration to someone with the same job title in a different company. This use of a Situation Slide is often called a "Reference Story".

Note: In a Vision Generation demonstration, if your Situation is on target and your customer gets really excited by your Illustration, then that is the <u>perfect</u> time to turn the conversation to a discussion of the customer's specific situation and needs—and hold the balance of the demonstration in reserve until you have completed sufficient qualification and diagnosis.

Strong Illustrations can be extremely valuable marketing collateral, if your customers share the need for similar Solutions. You can use your Illustrations in brochures, fact sheets, and on web sites, for example.

Organizations with multiple SE's often set up shared server areas to enable swapping and sharing of good Illustrations along with the related Situation Slides. The truly well organized company will realize that Illustrations and the accompanying Situation Slide information (job title, company, industry, CBI, Reasons, Specific Capabilities and the Delta) represents a critical knowledge asset. I strongly recommend that you capture and leverage this information across your Selling Teams.

Exercise: In your mind, review the last three demonstrations you gave or attended. What Illustrations would have knocked the audiences' socks off? Where are those socks today?

---

6. Develop The First Pass—The "Do It"

What is the most concise, most rational pathway to take from the beginning of a demonstration to get to the Illustration? What is the fewest number of mouse clicks required to go from launching your software to generating that screen that is the Illustration?

That's the "Do It".

The "Do It" pathway is the straight line. It is the shortest distance from launching your product to showing the Illustration. No extra explanations, no additional talking, no side trips. Just Do It.

The best "Do It" pathway shows the audience how <u>easy</u> it is to use your software. It demonstrates for them that:

1. Your software <u>can</u> indeed achieve the Illustration you showed—technical proof.

2. Your software is fast, easy and logical to use—emotional gratification.

How long should your "Do It" pathway be? Ask yourself the question another way: How <u>short</u> could it be? That's the pathway that you want to use.

Exercise: *Go to the market and come home.*

Did you take the shortest and fastest path? Would there have been any advantage for you to take longer?

Most "Do It" sections only take a minute or two to complete, and that's exactly what you want. A successful "Do It" proves that your product does offer the Specific Capabilities needed to generate the Illustration.

Try to end your "Do It" segment with the screen that shows the Illustration best. You've proven the Specific Capability and you want your audience to remember it.

Axiom: *Always end each segment with the best, most exciting screen possible. If it is the actual Illustration, then that's even better. This will be the last screen, the last image your audience will see—it will be the image they take home with them.*

Consider how long you are with your audience in a typical demonstration meeting: Thirty minutes? An hour? Perhaps two hours? Now consider how those few minutes compare with your audience's entire year: it is just a fraction of a percent of their total year's time.

Furthermore, consider the other inputs and messages your audience sees during a day, a week, a month, or a year. It is estimated that the typical person, today, sees approximately 3,000 "interruption-based" marketing messages every day—from television ads, billboards, email and web ads, etc.

When you see other people's demos, you may note that they walk through a long story and, finally, reach the big "payoff" screen—but then they only leave that screen up and visible for a few meager seconds! How can you be expected to really remember it well?

One solution is to summarize, repeatedly, with your most compelling, most powerful screen showing: the Illustration. Linger over it. Let your audience steep in it…! Leave it up while you field and address questions. Give your customer the best possible opportunities to let your Illustration sink in, be remembered, and retained.

A successful "Do It" also causes your audience to want to learn more. They'll say, "Can you show it in blue?" "Can I put a line over here?" "Can you include text from this report?" "Can I search and retrieve data from this source?"

These kinds of questions are Great Questions—they help to move the demo forward. These questions queue you up for your next section.

IMPORTANT! Remember to summarize at this point. After all, this is an important moment in the demo. You have proven one or more Specific Capabilities, and you need to call this out.

Do a brief summary: "So, we just ran through the few steps we need to create the report you need. We launched the software, created a query, executed a search and formatted the results in a table. Now let's do this again more slowly, and address the questions you raised."

Exercise: Count the number of mouse clicks it currently takes you to locate and open the files you use for typical demonstrations. If it sounds like you are running a sewing machine then you may want to re-organize where you place your files and how you access them!

Consider creating and placing icons on your desktop to enable you to launch applications and documents using the fewest number of mouse clicks.

It can often take a surprising number of clicks to navigate through file-open menus in order to reach the demonstration files or applications you want to show. Each click that the customer sees will be viewed by them as part of the process that the customer needs to follow in order to accomplish the task. Too many clicks will make it seem overly complex and challenging.

Keep it simple by organizing your demonstration files in top—or upper-level directories, or by putting appropriate icons on your desktop.

Exercise: *Think about the last few demos you have given or seen. How often do you find the file names "demo", "test", or similar constructs used? (Or "Demo1, Demo2, Demo3…?)*

Your objective is to generate a vision of the reality of the solution—so try to use as real-life a set of file names as possible.

At minimum, use the customer's name or company name for saving files and examples. Better yet, use the same format that the customer uses in their own work—ask them, at the appropriate time in the demo.

Using realistic file names helps to build the vision you are seeking to communicate.

Exercise: *Watch a colleague perform a demonstration (or ask a colleague to watch you when you demo). Arrange yourself so that you can only see the screen and __not__ their keyboard. Now track and monitor how often your colleague uses a keyboard shortcut (e.g., Ctrl-V for Edit-Paste).*

Ask yourself, "If I didn't know how to use this software, would I have understood what I was seeing when keyboard short-cuts are used?"

The point here is that using keyboard shortcuts can compromise your ability to generate a vision in the audience's mind of the __audience__ running the software for themselves.

Every time you use a shortcut you increase the risk of confusing your audience—because they literally did not __see__ how you moved from step to step.

Instead of using keyboard shortcuts, be deliberate and use the visible menu choices. That way, you'll help your audience build their own vision of seeing themselves running your software—and how easy it is to do it!

__Note:__ The Appendix includes a terrific example of Illustrations followed by "Do It" pathways—using Microsoft Publisher. You'll find it in Appendix 8.

---

7. Develop The Second Pass—The "Do It Again"

Your second pass through the software follows the "Do It" pathway, but now you can explore options, develop more details, and explain what you are doing more fully. The questions that you generated with audience members in the "Do It" can largely be answered in the "Do It Again" section.

The "Do It Again" pathway must still focus entirely on the Specific Capabilities needed by the customer for the Solution. Don't get distracted, don't show off capabilities that aren't relevant.

"Doing It Again" provides the opportunity for you to provide support for Specific Capabilities. You can show the breadth of Specific Capabilities. You can demonstrate how to address more complex examples—this is a great reason to create multiple Illustrations, by the way. You can explain the flexibility that your Specific Capabilities offer or provide, as long as it is relevant to the Solution.

As with the "Do It" pass, make sure to end the "Do It Again" segment with the strongest, most compelling Illustration screen you possibly can. Leave that screen up, as possible, while you do your brief summary and answer questions. The longer the audience sees that terrific screen, the better they will remember it.

What about the questions raised during the "Do It" pass? You can address Great Questions immediately in this section, but you want to defer Good Questions or Stupid Questions until the Question and Answer session towards the end. Hang on, we'll address the difference between Great, Good, and Stupid Questions and how to handle them in Chapter 9 Managing Time and Questions.

Axiom: *The "Do It" is the fastest route. The "Do It Again" is the scenic route.*

Axiom: *The first time you give a demo you'll generate a set of questions from audience members. The second time you present that same or similar demo to another, similar audience at a different site, you'll also generate a set of questions. Typically, there will be a healthy overlap in the questions between these two audiences—perhaps as much as an 80% overlap, in fact.*

Those questions that overlap between the two groups represent excellent feedstock for the content of your "Do It Again" pathway for the next demo to another, similar audience.

The clever reader will realize that only one initial demo will be needed to generate a reasonable set of questions from which good "Do It Again" material can be drawn…!

Presenting your Illustration(s) should be done in one or two minutes, or less. Running through your "Do It" should only take one or two minutes for reasonably straight-forward, individual Solutions.

From the audience's perspective, your "Do It Again" should feel complete but still concise. Five to ten minutes should be sufficient for most individual Solutions. The longer you take, the greater the risk that your software begins to appear to be too complex, or too hard to use, or that you present capabilities that aren't needed by the customer.

Your job is to fill them up and satisfy your audience without leaving them either hungry or overstuffed. Demos don't need doggy-bags!

When you have completed your "Do It Again" section be sure to summarize, again. You can use and expand upon the same Summary you used for the "Do It" section.

"We just completed all of the few steps you'll need to create the report you need. We launched the software, created a query that included three different types of search terms, executed a search and stored the results. We then generated a second query, ran that search and then merged the results of both searches together. We then formatted the results in a table, added images, and published the report to our colleagues via email."

So, here is your Great Demo! time-line so far, including Summaries:

Introduction	1-2 minutes
Illustration	1-2 minutes

Do It	1-2 minutes
Do It Again	5-10 minutes

Your total time presenting ranges from 8 to 16 minutes. Concise, targeted, effective. Surprisingly compelling, in fact!

You'll complete your demo with a Questions and Answers segment (more on this next chapter) and a final Summary.

A complete Great Demo! time-line might look like this:

Introduction	1-2 minutes
Illustration	1-2 minutes
Do It	1-2 minutes
Do It Again	5-10 minutes
Q & A	5-10 minutes
Summary	2-4 minutes

Look at that! Between 15 and 30 minutes for the entire performance—it's a Great Demo!

8. Practice

Now it's time to practice. (To be fair, most people either don't practice at all or only practice once to get a general feel for the demo, yet many people practice as often as they can and have time for. I recommend finding a "happy medium" with regards to practicing that fits your personality and skills…).

Your first objective in practicing your demo is to time it. You need to know how long the demo will take, without questions. Time this and then add an appropriate amount of time for questions that arise during your demo and for the actual Q & A session. In the example above, you'd estimate 5-10 minutes for the Q & A session plus 1-2 minutes for questions that come up during Illustration, "Do It", and "Do It Again" segments.

Then Review the Meeting Information Sheet to make sure that your demo plan fits the agenda you've agreed upon with the Salesperson. If it doesn't, most likely it will be too long. Rethink your "Do It Again" section and trim out items of lower priority.

It your demo is too short, review the Demonstration Information Sheet and see if you have missed any required Specific Capabilities. Check to make sure that your Illustration is truly powerful. If everything looks fine, then <u>leave your demo alone!</u> It's OK to finish early and give back time in the meeting.

Axiom: *Everybody loves meetings that finish early. They are surprised and pleased. It's a terrific way to differentiate yourself from the competition.*

Practice your demo one more time to make sure everything flows properly, to make sure that you don't run into any bugs, and to confirm that you complete in about the same amount of time. You might want to practice more, but hold off—it's time to get feedback from the team.

9. Present To The Selling Team

If you think an audience is tough to present to, just wait until you deliver your demo to the rest of the Selling Team! They'll want everything to be absolutely perfect, of course.

Axiom: *The <u>actual</u> amount of practice and Selling Team participation in preparing a demo is exactly proportional to the relative value of the deal.*

You <u>do</u> want to present the demo to the Selling Team, if at all possible. Often it is not realistic to do this for every demo (after all, you now have a great Earned Reputation for Great Demos!). Nevertheless, you'll find that Salespeople often want to see demos that have been prepared for large projects and big deals.

Present your demo exactly as if the balance of the Selling Team is the audience. A rehearsal style session that includes all members of the Selling Team, playing their roles, is the best way to practice. That way, everyone adjusts their verbal presentations to match one another and link the meeting together. The balance of the Team should play members of the expected audience.

Take feedback. Listen and itemize any changes or improvements that are agreed upon. The whole Selling Team has a lot at stake—everyone wants the upcoming meeting with the customer to be a success.

Be careful, however, to limit the demo to the Specific Capabilities defined. The Selling Team, as a whole, must resist the temptation to add capabilities to the demo. Keep focused!

Once you have completed presenting the demo and taking feedback, review specifically what changes you will make. If you can make the desired changes right during the rehearsal, then do so and repeat the rehearsal. If you don't have time or can't make the changes "on the fly", make sure that you are all in agreement regarding both the specific changes <u>and</u> the overall timeline for the meeting, including the demo portion.

10. Adjust And Refine

Make any agreed-upon changes that came from the rehearsal. If your Illustration(s) changed, then you'll need to redo both the "Do It" and "Do It Again" segments that produce the changed Illustration(s).

If the "Do It" section has changed, then you'll need to adjust the "Do It" and most likely you'll also have to change the "Do It Again" segment.

Axiom: *The Chain of Pain applies to the cascade from the Illustration to the "Do It" to the "Do It Again".*

Once you've made your changes, practice your demo again for timing and make sure it fits in the meeting agenda. When everything fits correctly, you may be ready to go.

How do I know when I have practiced enough? Tough question! The best answer is: You are ready when your demo is memorized, addresses the required Specific Capabilities, and fits the time allotted.

A pragmatic answer is that you are ready when you have practiced enough that you feel confident. The amount of practice you need will depend on your familiarity with the software, the complexity of the demo, and the length of the demo.

What about a script? A script is a crutch—it is tough to run a race with a crutch. On the other hand, a crutch may be exactly what you need to get across the finish line. Avoid using one if you can. If you must, well, then you must. It is better to use a script and execute the demo well, than to try to memorize a long, complex demo and make mistakes.

When you have practiced enough and are confident, then you are nearly ready to go.

11. Confirm Infrastructure With The Customer

It is likely that a few days, or possibly even several weeks, have passed since you contacted the customer in step 2.

Axiom: *No surprises. Really.*

Before you get on that airplane, in the car, or board that train to go to your customer's site, give them a call. Confirm that the infrastructure you agreed upon is going to be ready. This is one final chance to head off infrastructure-based problems.

Review your Infrastructure Checklist and re-confirm that everything you need will be ready and waiting. Double check on any equipment that you will be renting—now is the time to pick it up, if possible, and familiarize yourself with its operation and compatibility with your computer.

There are three additional questions you should consider asking, as well:

1. Have any of the objectives for the meeting changed?

2. Are there any new participants in the audience?

3. Are there any new time constraints or limitations?

How many times have you started a demonstration meeting and had your customer say, "I'm sorry, but we now only have thirty minutes, instead of the two hours we'd originally planned upon…"

Asking these key questions a day or two ahead of the demo meeting gives you a fighting chance to make adjustments or changes. This is <u>much</u> better than the alternative of learning of changes at the start of the meeting, itself!

OK—you are ready to roll!

By the way, don't be surprised if you receive applause after you complete your Great Demo…!

But—What If You Don't Know Your Product Well?

It is quite possible that you may have situations where you don't know your product in great detail. Here are a few example cases:

- The product is extremely new (Alpha, Beta, or other new versions or new releases).

- The product was purchased from a third party and is now sold by your company.

- You just joined the company and all of the offerings are new, to you.

In any situation where you are the technical resource, ultimately responsible for detailed understanding of your software products, you have two choices, initially:

1. Work <u>very</u> hard and learn the product <u>very</u> rapidly!

2. Use or make a Canned Demo.

If you do use a Canned Demo and you are the technical resource, you'll eventually have to learn your product intimately, anyway. For you, a Canned Demo is only an interim fix—a Band-Aid.

For the non-technical folks, a Canned Demo may be the safest strategy for you. It is your choice, of course, whether to invest the time required to really learn your product in sufficient detail to deliver a credible demo. The issue here boils down to how well know your audience's CBI's, Reasons, and Specific Capabilities—how well they have been qualified. If the Specific Capabilities are well defined and clear, it will always be easier to deliver a credible demo—or a Great Demo! The less qualified the audience, the greater the need to know all capabilities and aspects of your offerings.

For more on Canned Demos, see Chapter 10 "Special Situations". The section on Canned Demos provides a number of options and strategies that may be available to you, based on your specific type of product and your situation.

The Summary is the same for all situations—whether you know the product or don't know the product well—the audience's main interest is in seeing the Specific Capabilities they need to address their CBI's. That is <u>always</u> a key element of a Great Demo!

Eleven Steps To Success

Following these eleven steps is an investment in your success and in the success of your organization. They will guide you through preparing for your demonstrations and provide you with the greatest possible opportunity for success.

For now, you might consider memorizing these eleven steps, or printing them out and posting them in your work area as a reminder. Use them as a checklist:

1. Execute Research.

2. Coordinate Infrastructure with customer.

3. Create your Outline.

4. Create your Summary and Introduction.

5. Create your Illustration.

6. Develop the first pass (the "Do It").

7. Develop the second pass (the "Do It Again").

8. Practice.

9. Present to the Selling Team.

10. Adjust and Refine.

11. Confirm infrastructure with customer

I'd suggest that you follow these steps religiously until they become second nature for you!

Note: The Appendix includes a terrific example of a Great Demo!—using Microsoft Word as the example product. You'll find it in Appendix 9.

9
Managing Time and Questions

Handling Questions

There are three types of questions that arise in demos:

1. Great Questions (that should be answered right away)

2. Good Questions (that should be answered later)

3. Stupid Questions (that need to be answered even though they never should have been asked)

I'll provide you with methods for handling all three types of questions. Equally, if not more important, I'll help you manage your audience so that the flow of your demo is not broken or derailed.

Axiom: *The more technical the audience the more type 2 "Good Questions (that should be answered later)" and type 3 "Stupid Questions" you'll receive.*

Let's address each class of questions separately.

Great Questions (That Should Be Answered Right Away)

What is a Great Question that needs an immediate response? (That's a good question in its own right!) These Great Questions are questions that directly impact the Specific Capabilities that are needed by the customer <u>and</u> are relevant to the Specific Capabilities being demonstrated. These questions need to be addressed right away.

These questions, and their answers, support your demo and help to underscore your major points. Answering them immediately will not only help the flow but will enhance the perceived value of your product.

A terrific example of a Great Question is any question that leads to your next screen or next few screens. These Great Questions almost make it seem like you have a person planted in the audience! Note—it is a good idea to reward these apparent "shills" verbally, with praise or a joke. You'll increase their emotional level of support as a result, since they become part of the "team".

What is a good answer to a Great Question? (That's another good question!) A good answer is brief and directly to the point. In the "shill" example above, a good answer could be "I'm really glad you asked that question—that's the next capability I'd planned to share with you." [Joke potential: "…and that's another $20 I owe you!" or "Thank you for leading the witness…"]

Most Great Questions will not necessarily lead you to the next segment of your demo, but certainly deserve a crisp and positive response. Keep your answer focused and brief. Use whatever explanation is required, but do not draw it out. If you feel you need to spend more than two sentences on the answer then you don't have a Great Question, you are dealing with a Good Question instead. You can actually feel the difference as you respond!

Is it OK to respond with a simple "Yes" or "No"?

Yes, it is.

In fact, a simple "Yes" or "No" answer may be all that your audience wants or needs.

"Does it run on NT?"
"Yes."

"Can I apply different line styles?"
"Yes"

"Is your product expensive?"
"No."

Exercise: *Ask your spouse or significant other if they love you. Do you want more than a yes or no answer?*

Exercise: *If your spouse or significant other asks if you love him/her, does she/he want more than a yes or no answer? If the answer is anything other than yes, what happens?*

The point here is that very often you can answer a critical question with a simple yes or no answer. Your customer will generally let you know if they want additional discussion or proof. If you can answer a key question with a strong and confident "yes", and that satisfies the customer, then you are done with that issue. Clamp your mouth shut and say nothing further on the topic.

You do need to be careful that you are not perceived as being flippant with a simple "yes" or "no" response. Either be sure or ask—it is perfectly OK to ask, "It that sufficient, or would you like more information?" As your experience grows you'll be able to discern which questions can be handled with "yes" or "no" responses versus those that require a sentence or two of more detailed explanation.

Great Questions are opportunities for you to support your demo and/ or to move it forward. *Cave Occasio!*

Axiom: Liars are <u>always</u> caught out. As a technical representative or repre- sentative of the capabilities of your software, you can <u>never</u> lie. This is your personal code of honor, your professional position, your general code of eth- ics. Lying to get a sale will lose you the next, and the next, and the next....

Good Questions (That Should Be Answered Later)

Most questions fall into this category. They are truly Good Questions that deserve a considered response. Traditionally, the challenge for you is to determine how to answer this question adequately without derail- ing your demonstration or boring the balance of the audience.

Good Questions are the single greatest risk to your Great Demo! This is not because they are necessarily hard questions or beyond your expertise. It is because once you've launched into your explanation you risk the following real possibilities:

1. You risk additional follow-up questions on the same topic that will drive the demo down a side road (sometimes it may be a dead-end road!). The further down this road you venture, the higher the risk of "losing" the balance of your audience. Once distracted, they will begin to talk amongst themselves—and then you've lost control of your audience. Recovering can be very difficult.

2. You risk having members of your audience enter into a side discussion on the topic. It may be an issue that they have been discussing for months, and you've just re-opened it for them. And once a side discussion has begun, it causes others to begin. Recovering from this can be even more challenging.

3. At minimum you risk boring other (potentially key) members of your audience, who may not be interested in the particular issue.

Any of these three possibilities is not good. How do you manage this problem?

Anecdote: I once gave a demo where a simple question was asked, "Does it run on Oracle?" Notwithstanding my brief response, it turned out that there was a furious debate ongoing in the customer's organization between choosing Oracle versus Ingres. A truly pointless discussion ensued between two members of the audience—an argument, really.

It was clear that these two people would have been happy to continue to debate the relative merits of Oracle versus Ingres for the next hour. This would have been disastrous for my demo. I was able to park their argument and get back on track using the following technique.

The "Not Now" List

Your solution is called the "Not Now" List. It is simple and effective to apply.

When you are asked a Good Question, you simply reply with following:

> "That's an excellent question. I promise to address it, but for right now I'd like to continue with our meeting plan. Let me write it down, here, on the whiteboard. [You write down the question, in brief.] We'll make sure to address it later. Is that OK with you?"

There are four key points to doing this successfully.

1. First, you must honestly acknowledge the question. This must be earnest and perceived by your audience as sincere. If your audience feels that you are "blowing them off" then you have failed, and must answer the question immediately.

2. Second, write the question down for public display. This could be a whiteboard, a flipchart, or you can even a Microsoft Word document that you create on-the-fly. In any case, it needs to be captured clearly and succinctly, and captured such that the person that asked the question is convinced that you understand the question and will indeed answer it.

3. Your response, "Is that OK with you?" is also very important. This provides the opportunity for the questioner to be satisfied for the present and to indicate his or her willingness to postpone the answer. Another example phrase you can use is:

   "Excellent question. In the interest of time, can I write it down over here, for now, and continue? [Audience member responds, "Yes."] We'll make sure to answer your question later."

   This example also allows your questioner to participate in the decision to postpone the answer. This ability to participate in the decision is important and is a key to making this work well.

4. You MUST remember to answer the question at the appropriate time (most typically in the Question and Answer portion of the demonstration time). I'll discuss this further, below. Failing to answer the question, ultimately, will leave the questioner with an open issue that can fester and come back to hurt your sale. ALWAYS gain closure with questions.

Now you can see why this is called the "Not Now" List! As you go through your demo and receive Good Questions from the audience, add them to the Not Now List. It is quite possible that by the end of your demo you may have a half a dozen questions on your Not Now List. They are all nicely queued up and ready for you. But—when do you finally answer them? Hang on, we'll get to that in a moment.

Anecdote: *Remember the old elementary school joke, "How do you keep an idiot in suspense?" The annoying answer was "I'll tell you later...!"*

Stupid Questions (That Need To Be Answered Even Though They Never Should Have Been Asked)

Stupid Questions are an excellent opportunity for you to shine and show your professionalism. Stupid questions arise from two sources, typically:

1. Audience members who are trying to show off their technical knowledge or who are trying to trip you up. They may be decidedly hostile: they don't like you; they don't like your product; they don't like your company.

2. Audience members who really don't understand. (Dilbert's Pointy-Headed Boss, for example).

Both types of people do exist and do show up as members of your audiences. There are often people who take real pleasure in attempting to "stump" the vendor expert (that's you). They like to throw curve balls. They want to see you squirm. Don't let 'em. Here's how:

It's very simple: treat every Stupid Question with the same respect, same attention, and same professionalism as you do with Good Questions. In fact, every Stupid Question <u>must</u> be treated as a Good Question. For you, there are no Stupid Questions.

Manage Stupid Questions using the Not Now List. Queue them up along with the Good Questions. You'll gain respect from the balance of the audience for your professional manner. Note, also, that many Stupid Questions are from audience members who would like nothing more than to derail you. By treating their questions respectfully and by providing them with equal billing on the Not Now List, they necessarily will be satisfied and silenced for the moment. The rest of the audience who really is interested in your demo will be pleased and grateful.

The Moral: There are only Great Questions and Good Questions, as far as you are concerned.

Addressing The Not Now List

When <u>do</u> you answer the questions on the Not Now List? Let's recall our plan for Great Demos:

Strategy For A Single-Solution Demonstration:

1. Introduction

2. Present the Illustration—Summarize

3. Do It—Summarize

4. Do It Again—Summarize

5. Questions & Answers

6. Summarize

Strategy For A Multiple-Solution Demonstration:

1. Introduction

2. Briefly Present All Illustrations—Summarize

3. Then, For Each Solution:

    a. Present the Illustration—Summarize

    b. Do It—Summarize

    c.   Do It Again—Summarize

4.   Questions & Answers

5.   Summarize

Ah ha! You answer all remaining questions (i.e., Good Questions and Stupid Questions) in the Questions and Answers section, after your have completed your summary for the last "Do It Again" portion of the demonstration.

However, it is possible that not everyone is interested working through the list of questions. Depending on how the meeting is structured, you can offer a choice: stay or leave.

If the agenda for the overall meeting has the demonstration as the last item, you can summarize after the last "Do It Again" and then let everyone know that you will address the questions on the Not Now List. You can then invite those who are interested to stay, and those who are satisfied can either stay or leave as they choose.

This is an important step. You are providing audience members who are satisfied, who are already convinced that your offering has the Specific Capabilities they need to solve their Critical Business Issues (CBI's), with the opportunity to get back to work and save time. By definition, it reduces the remaining audience to those people who are sincerely interested in having their specific questions answered.

Very often, the people who were trying to derail you will leave at this point. You <u>still</u> need to answer their question(s), but it seriously reduces their issues' importance relative to the other, earnest questions.

This controlled "triage" of audience at this point also provides opportunities for your Salesperson to engage in follow-up discussions with the key members of the audience.

Finally, it leaves you with the audience who is seriously interested in your product. Thus it becomes the natural selection of the people who are most likely to become the key users and power users of your product.

Axiom: *Did I mention no surprises?*

Make sure that your invitation to stay or leave is not a surprise for the balance of the Selling Team! You'll want to make sure that the Team, and the Salesperson in particular, is in agreement with strategy. Plan to discuss and include this as an option when defining the meeting agenda.

Answering Questions—The Process

Answering questions has a protocol for success, just like other actions in your Great Demo! The simple process is as follows:

1. Restate the question—ask if you understand it correctly.

2. Provide the answer—crisply—but sufficiently.

3. Summarize both the question and the answer.

Restating each question provides you with two important opportunities. The first is that it enables you to identify (or re-identify) the person who asked the question. The advantage of this is that you can direct your answer to that person, in a more one-to-one dialog fashion. This personalizes your response and any follow-up questions that arise, as well.

Here's a Q and A typical scenario, using our Great Demo! technique:

> The Question as written on the Not Now List: "What are the support policies for operating systems?"

Restate the Question: "If I understand correctly, you want to know about our support policies for various operating systems—when do we stop support or begin support, for example—is that right?"

Audience Member Response: "Yes, in particular I'm concerned about your plans for supporting Windows 98. We have a number of users still on Windows 98 and I need to know if we will be able to support them."

The Answer: "Yes, we do currently support Windows 98, along with the current released versions of Windows. Our policy is to support the current version of Windows, plus one version behind the current. We do give customers 12 months notice before we stop support of any operating system or hardware platform. As new versions of Windows, for example, appear from Microsoft, we get Beta copies for our internal testing. We are generally able to announce support for new versions of mainstream operating systems and hardware at the same time they are released publicly."

Summary: "So, we do support Windows 98 today and expect to continue support for the next 12 months, at least. We can provide you with our complete listing of supported operating systems and hardware, if you'd like."

Audience Member: "Terrific. All we really need is to be able to support Win 98 for the next several months. Great Demo…!"

As always, it is important to summarize. In fact, the longer and more complex the question, resulting discussion and answer, the more important it is to recall the question and crisply review the answer.

Can You Show Me?

Often, verbal answers to questions are satisfactory for your audience. Equally often, however, they want or expect you to show them on the computer. After all, a demonstration is typically presented to offer proof of capabilities. Being asked to "Show me" is fair and reasonable.

"Show Me" situations come in two possible flavors:

1. You can show the Specific Capabilities needed to address the question.

2. You can't.

Let's examine what to do in both cases.

You Can

In the first situation, you know that you can indeed present the Specific Capabilities needed to address the question, and the audience does want to see it demonstrated. Guess what? This is an opportunity for a mini-version of a Great Demo! All of the skills and processes we've discussed apply directly. So do it! What do you do?

1. Present the Illustration—Summarize

2. Do It—Summarize

3. Do It Again—Summarize

4. Q & A.

5. Summarize

Obviously, your mini-Great Demo! will be shorter than your full demo—it may only be one or two minutes long. Nevertheless, by applying the same principles you'll ensure that you address the question to your audience's satisfaction. Additionally, you'll do it with the minimum amount of time and steps necessary to close the issue.

A note—you can test at each step is your audience is satisfied or wants to pursue into more detail. For example, the Illustration alone may be sufficient to close the question. If so, you're done! Summarize and return to the Not Now List of questions. If you need to go deeper, no problem. Go as far as necessary, testing at each level to see if you have closed the question satisfactorily. When you have the question adequately addressed, summarize and return to the Not Now List.

You Can't

There may be a number of reasons why you can't demonstrate the Specific Capability requested or necessary to answer the question. Your actions and responses are a bit like an "If Then" list:

If: Your software does have the capability, but it is unavailable to be demonstrated at this specific time or session,

Then: Say so. Let your audience know that your offering can indeed do what is required. Your positive response may be all that is required. If they want more proof, you can try to describe using static tools—product brochures, web pages, etc. You can even try to outline what your product does on a whiteboard. If a real, live demonstration is required, then you need to set up a follow-up visit or opportunity to demonstrate this Specific Capability.

If: Your software does not have the capability, period,

Then: Say so. If you can offer an alternative capability that may be sufficient, then present it. If you have nothing to offer in your current offering, then you need to test the importance of the capability. Is it a "nice to have" capability or is it a Specific Capability truly needed to solve a CBI?

In the case where the capability is a "nice to have" situation, then you can offer to sponsor that capability to your Development group for inclusion in a future release.

In the case where the capability is really a Specific Capability necessary to close the sale, then your responsibilities are two-fold: First, make sure that your Salesperson is made clearly aware of the situation. This provides your company the ability to assign a real value to that Specific Capability and prioritize it for Development. Second, you need to carefully capture the customer's situation and gain as clear an understanding of the Specific Capability as possible—how it will be used, how it should manifest, etc.—and accurately report the information to your Development group and process.

Is this a failure? Possibly, if your competition can offer all of the other necessary Specific Capabilities as well as this particular Specific Capability. All other things being equal, your competition would get the order in this case.

However, it is likely that no one product is a perfect fit for the customer. Your product may include 80% of the desired Specific Capabilities; your competition's product may offer a different 80% of the desired Specific Capabilities.

By following the process above, you have the opportunity to differentiate yourself from the competition (unless they read this book as well!), by working to really understand the new Specific Capability needed for the sale. If the customer is confident in you and your ability to sponsor the importance and resolution of new development work, then the customer may choose to purchase your product under the expectation that the new Specific Capability will be developed and released in a satisfactory time-frame.

In particular, if you have spent time side-by-side with the customer to understand the desired Specific Capability and have developed a vision together of how it should manifest, then your customer will tend to support your cause. This will be even stronger if your competition does not invest the time to clearly understand the required new Specific Capability.

Anecdote: A Salesperson was known, in his early days, to often ask the question, "If we had it would you buy it?"

Can You Run My Example?

What do you do if an audience member wants to run one of his or her own examples? Let's say that you've completed most of a Great Demo!

and are handling questions. Someone asks if you can try working an example, real-life problem.

This is an absolutely terrific opportunity!

In the Q & A period, you certainly should run specific customers examples, if appropriate, and if you are confident that the results will be positive.

The key to success here is to set expectations very carefully! After all, their examples are, by definition, unrehearsed. In a database search, for example, you might find no answers or only inappropriate answers. You might uncover a bug. You might even crash.

So set expectations carefully. Start at zero and build upwards. Depending on what is appropriate for the situation, you may want to state any or all of the possible outcomes from running their example. Let them know what <u>might</u> happen, so that if something bad <u>does</u> happen, everyone is prepared.

However, if you have a success, well then, you are <u>Golden!</u> When successful, this can be VERY effective. People LOVE to actually take something useful away from a demo.

That's an extremely powerful concept. Most demos are just that—a demo. No real data, at least not data that addresses specific problems. If members of your audience leave with real results, useful information, and solutions to real problems, then you have not only nailed the technical sale but you've generated a set of extremely strong supporters. You've made the time they invested in your demo truly productive and proved that they will get value out of using your product right away.

Clearly, any real examples that you prepare ahead of time are also important, as described in Chapter 8, Technical Preparation. Nevertheless, your ability to successfully execute their examples *ad hoc* will truly make the event a Great Demo!

Axiom: *Finding no results in a search can, strangely enough, be a big positive.*

This is not necessarily intuitive, but it can be very powerful when presented logically.

Let's say that you offer a product that enables your customer to search a database filled with relevant content. In a demo meeting, the customer asks you to do a specific search. You create a logical query, execute the search, and find nothing.

Most people will initially be disappointed—however, you can point out that the <u>negative</u> results can be just as important as positive results. The fact that nothing was found in the database can mean:

- *The information they are looking for is truly new (patent, product, or publishing opportunity!).*

- *They don't have to search over that same content using their old tools—to find the same negative result.*

- *The time spent doing the search with your offering, to find the negative result, may have been <u>much</u> faster than what it would have taken to find the same results previously.*

These benefits can help you turn a negative into a positive result.

Any Other Questions?

Often, Q & A sessions can become rather interactive, and this is great, particularly since it integrates you with the audience. Once you believe you have addressed all of the questions on the Not Now List, as well as any others that come up during Q & A, you need to ask if there are any further questions.

Address these directly, as appropriate. If there appear to be several, you may want to use the Not Now List as a tool to organize and queue these additional questions.

Closing Q & A

Just as with every other part of a Great Demo!, you need to properly close the Q & A session. You do this by summarizing. You briefly review each of the questions from the Not Now List, and provide a very brief summary of the answer for each one. It can be very effective to put check marks (✓) after each question as you complete it. Make sure that you have adequately addressed all of the questions from the Not Now List.

Be sure to highlight any requests for new capabilities or Specific Capabilities, and your promised action steps for follow-up. And, be sure to also call attention to any *ad hoc* successful examples you ran on behalf of your audience.

Finally, thank everyone for coming and for staying through the Q & A session. Make sure that audience members who may want to contact you have your card or contact information.

Demonstration Roadmaps

We've explored a range of tools and techniques to help address managing questions and time in demonstrations. As your demos grow more complex and include more sets of Solutions and Specific Capabilities, you may run the risk of losing your audience due to them getting lost or confused. The Demonstration Roadmap is an excellent tool to help you keep your audience on track and focused.

The Demonstration Roadmap is essentially an expanded form of an agenda. It can be, in fact, your Outline—the same outline you generated when you began to prepare your demonstration—and your agenda. The critical difference is that you create your Outline for your-self, and you put together a Roadmap for the benefit of your audience.

Axiom: *Outline = Agenda = Demonstration Roadmap.*

You can create a Demonstration Roadmap using a number of tools, including Microsoft Word, PowerPoint, or other software products. Whichever you choose, the essence is to use a tool that you can either leave in view, such as an overhead, or that you can flip back and forth between your actual demonstration and the Roadmap.

Creating your Roadmap in PowerPoint is a terrific solution. This pro-vides you with the added advantage of including the Roadmap as a part of an overall presentation. You can easily toggle between a PowerPoint slide and your demonstration as desired.

Exercise: *Create a slide in PowerPoint with your Outline. Change to Slide-Show mode. Now make sure that your demo will still run properly as you toggle back and forth between segments of your demonstration and PowerPoint in Slide-Show mode with your Roadmap up.*

You'll want to make sure that this executes smoothly and does not introduce any new bugs or problems.

The process to create a simple Roadmap is easy. Begin with typing or copying your Outline into an appropriate PowerPoint slide (your cor-porate background, etc.). Now rephrase the individual bullet items to be clear and customer-oriented. For example, here is a simple Outline from earlier in our work:

1. Introduction.

2. Present the Illustrations for all Solutions.

3. For Each Solution,

    a. Re-present the Illustration for that Solution.

    b. Rapidly demonstrate that set of Specific Capabilities. Follow with a brief summary.

    c. Walk more deliberately through demonstrating that set of Specific Capabilities. Summarize for that set of Specific Capabilities.

4. Summarize for <u>all</u> sets of Specific Capabilities.

5. Questions and Answers.

6. Final Summary.

If you plan to have two Solutions, then your Roadmap might look like:

- Introduction
- Overview of Both Solutions
- Solution Number 1
    - Illustration
    - Overview of Specific Capabilities
    - Detail of Specific Capabilities
- Solution Number 2
    - Illustration
    - Overview of Specific Capabilities
    - Detail of Specific Capabilities
- Summary
- Questions and Answers
- Final Summary

As you move through your demonstration and complete each major segment, you can use PowerPoint's various Animation tools to help keep your audience oriented. For example, after you demonstrate the first Solution, you toggle back to your PowerPoint Roadmap slide and have a checkmark (✓) appear next to the first Solution item. You can also "dim" the previous items to help highlight where you are on the roadmap.

Roadmaps can be simple bulleted text lists, as above, or even show a real "roadmap", with lines and boxes to help organize and define sections of your demo. It's your choice how complex you'd like your Roadmap to become, but remember that the whole objective of the Roadmap is to provide clarity!

Axiom: In Switzerland, there is a saying, with regards to their annual Carnival, "Now we are going to have chaos, and this is how we are going to organize it!"

The Roadmap can also help when you do your Summary and Final Summary, following Questions and Answers. You can use the Roadmap as a template to review and summarize for each Solution or set of Specific Capabilities.

You Are Now Ready...

That's it! That's everything you need to create and execute a truly Great Demo! Now get out there and generate some business!

Axiom: What did you sell today?

10

Special Situations

An alternative title for this chapter might be "Real-Life Situations". The process we've developed so far works extremely well for well-qualified Technical Proof demos. However, we all know that the one thing you should expect in a sales process is the unexpected...!

There are many types of special situations that present additional challenges to delivering Great Demos, or even moderately successful demos. It is even possible that you encounter more special situation demos than "normal" demonstrations. You can, however, control and these more challenging situations to a successful conclusion by following the principles we have explored so far.

Here are a set of special situations that we will examine:

- The "Elevator" Demo
- Generic Demos (e.g., Marketing demos)
- Vision Generation
- Trade show Demos
- Dealing with large, unqualified groups
- Demos for product roll-outs
- Remote Demos
- Canned Demos

- Scripted Demos

- Deployment Demos

We'll provide tools and expand the method we've explored so far to increase your probability of addressing these scenarios successfully.

DemoGurus, the community website at www.DemoGurus.com, offers up-to-date information, tips, best practices and tools for handling the broad range of situations that you may encounter in real-life situations.

The "Elevator" Demo

Imagine that you are at a conference and you step into an elevator. Inside is the Vice President of the company that your team has been working on a large order for a year. Your Salesperson has never been able to meet with this VP. Now, all of a sudden, you have the opportunity of the year! (Don't blow it!) The VP looks at your conference badge and says, "Hmmm, your company looks familiar, tell me, what do your products do?"

This is it! You've got literally seconds to answer him, before the elevator gets to his floor. What do you say?

The "elevator pitch" is well known in the sales world. Salespeople practice condensing all of the offerings and capabilities of their company into one or two concise, crystal-clear statements. These few statements summarize and highlight the most important, highest value deliverables that your company provides. Remember, you may have only fifteen seconds before the door opens and he gets out!

Exercise: Write down, in one concise sentence, what your company does. Now read it back to yourself and ask yourself the following question, "Would I want to learn more?"

If your answer is no, then try writing it again, differently, and again, until you get so excited that you call your Salesperson and place an order yourself!

Here's a (poor) example:

> You: "We provide software and services to the pharmaceutical industry."

Yawn. Boring. Goodbye, Mr. VP. Let's try again. What is the most important, most commonly used set of capabilities that are sold by your company? How are those capabilities used most often by your customers? What applications or Solutions do those capabilities address? That information provides the raw material for a successful elevator pitch.

Here is the same example, revisited:

> You: "We help pharmaceutical companies increase their number of successful drug candidates by enabling scientists to access all of the information they need to make better, faster decisions—and decisions they couldn't make before."
>
> VP: "Really? Do you have a card?"

Much better! But…this is the same kind of statement that your Salesperson would make. What does it have to do with a demo? The answer is two-fold.

First, you and your company's ability to crystallize the most important core capabilities, applications, and solutions is the key to creating good marketing demos. We'll explore this in the next section. Hang on…

Second, notice that he asked you for a card. If you are going to have to bend down and open your brief case, why not provide him with something that really stands out? Give him a selection of your best Illustrations, along with your card.

Now he has both your verbal description, which caught his attention, <u>and</u> paper copies of the highest value, knock-your-socks-off deliverables that your company offers! You've created an opportunity that has a reasonable likelihood of paying off. He may decide to take a personal interest in the project and call you (don't be surprised). Or, he may delegate a lieutenant to contact you to pursue how the Illustrations were created. Your job in both cases is to make sure that your Salesperson is integrated into the loop rapidly.

Always carry copies of your best Illustrations with you. You never know when you may meet a customer…

Generic Demos

While one of the key points of this book is to avoid doing unqualified demos, it is highly likely that you'll still have to do them. That being the case, what can we do to increase the probability of success in situations where you have little or no information about your customer?

These unqualified demos, or Generic Demos, can come from many quarters:

- Trade shows
- On-the-fly events
- Webinar demos
- "Vision Generation" meetings
- Demos for analysts
- Demos for third parties

While each Generic Demo situation may be unique, there are common denominators between them. First, by definition, the audience is unqualified or relatively unqualified. You have no clear idea or confirmation of any Critical Business Issues (CBI's), Reasons, or Specific Capabilities. Second, you may have no understanding of the relationship, if any, between members of the audience. These two conditions make it tough to make a successful connection between their (unknown) business issues and your capabilities.

What can you do?

If you have the opportunity, ask questions. Asking questions and uncovering even basic qualification information may give you enough data to substantially increase your odds of success. If you are able to learn enough, and are lucky, you may be able to turn a Generic Demo into a Great Demo!

However, if you are unable to gather sufficient information, then you really have to deliver a Generic Demo. The best Generic Demos present your product's key, most valuable capabilities. These are the capabilities that are purchased most often, or more accurately, these capabilities are the reason why your software was purchased by your existing customers.

This is really the same situation as the Elevator Demo, and you can use a similar process to construct the outline for a Generic Demo.

Exercise: "Why <u>did</u> they buy?"

Sit down with one or more Salespeople (more is better). Have them outline their past 3-5 successful product sales, and for each sale identify the CBI, Reasons, and Specific Capabilities. Use a whiteboard and group the closely related CBI's, Reasons, and Specific Capabilities together.

(You can get a head start by going back to Chapter 4 and finding the exercise that provided you with information on why your customers purchased your products, and begin with this information.)

Next, track down the Illustrations that were used for each successful sale, and group the Illustrations according to the CBI's above. You should find that your CBI's and Specific Capabilities cluster reasonably tightly for each product, application, and market.

Each of these clusters has the information you need to create Generic Demos for each product, application and market area.

This is called a "Why did they buy?" session and it may differ substantially from tradition marketing approaches. Most typically, marketing teams think in terms of the future and the subjunctive mood (sorry!): "Why do we think they should buy?"

A strong recommendation is to put a plan in place that causes a sales and/or marketing representative in your organization to go back to each customer some number of months after that customer purchases and implements your product. You will want to interview your customer to learn:

- *Why did they purchase your product?*

- *What problems and CBI's were they trying to address? What were the Reasons and Specific Capabilities they needed?*

- *How are they using your product today? What problems and CBI's are they successfully addressing using your offering?*

- *What unanticipated problems and CBI's are they also addressing with your product (this one can be really exciting!)?*

- *What value are they actually receiving from using your offering (real-life Delta information—stunningly important!)?*

This information becomes your Reference Stories (Situation Slides) for the next sale, and the next, and the next. You should make these interviews a standard practice after each sale is completed and your product is implemented into production use.

Axiom: Many companies do sales "loss" analysis; very few do "win" analysis—but they should!

This is, in fact, a marketing exercise. However, if you don't have a marketing department, or don't have time to wait for them to put a set of Generic Demos together, then you must do it yourself. In any case, now it is simple to create your Generic Demos.

From the exercise above, you have a set of Situation Slides, Illustrations and the Specific Capabilities used to create each Illustration. You now follow the same process you used in Chapter 8, Technical Preparation, to create your Generic Demo in the same format as if it were going to be a Great Demo!

While similar, the process for building a Generic Demo is somewhat different from that of a Great Demo! Here are the steps we followed in preparing a Great Demo!:

1. Execute Research.

2. Coordinate Infrastructure with customer.

3. Create your Outline.

4. Create your Summary and Introduction.

5. Create your Illustration.

6. Develop the first pass (the "Do It").

7. Develop the second pass (the "Do It Again").

8. Practice.

9. Present to the Selling Team.

10. Adjust and Refine.

11. Confirm infrastructure with customer

Clearly, many of these steps are not relevant or are simply impossible in Generic Demo Situations. The steps then are changed to the following for a Generic Demo:

1. Execute general Research. Use the Exercise above to generate the desired information, and/or gather what is already available from Marketing. Since you have no access to your customer to qualify, you can't do any real customer-specific research.

2. Create your Outline.

3. Create your Summary and Introduction.

4. Create your Illustration. Existing Situation Slides (now used as Reference Stories) and Illustrations may be perfect. However, make sure that there is no specific or confidential customer information presented. This needs to be cleaned out and replaced with generic data.

5. Develop the first pass (the "Do It").

6. Develop the second pass (the "Do It Again").

7. Practice.

8. Present to the Selling Team. Better yet, present to a group of Salespeople and SE's for feedback.

9. Adjust and Refine.

10. Print out copies of the Illustrations and keep them with you.

Optimally, building a representative set of Generic Demos is the task of Marketing. Even if you feel you don't have sufficient time to wait for marketing to create a suite of Generic Demos, you may need their help in creating "dummy" data sets or other demonstration files. Even better, ask your marketing colleagues to purchase a copy of this book and then they can learn to build both Generic Demos and Great Demos themselves (and provide them to you)!

Axiom: *"Give a man a fish and you feed him for a day. Teach a man to fish and you feed him for a lifetime."*
—*Proverb.*

Once your Generic Demos are completed, you can use them for a range of special situations. Here is the summarized list of items for creating Generic Demos:

1. Execute general Research.

2. Create your Outline.

3. Create your Summary and Introduction.

4. Create your Illustration.

5. Develop the first pass (the "Do It").

6. Develop the second pass (the "Do It Again").

7. Practice.

8. Present to the Selling Team.

9. Adjust and Refine.

10. Prepare copies of the Illustrations.

Vision Generation

There is an interesting expression that states, "You see it, but the customer does not". This means that your Salesperson or Selling Team understands that a customer has a Critical Business Issue that needs to be addressed, but the customer has yet to realize it.

Exercise: *Imagine a situation in day-to-day life where someone has a problem but is not aware of it. Write it down and also write down a solution to the problem.*

Here's an example: A company colleague leaves work at the end of the day. Since it is getting dark he turns his car lights on, but his taillights are out—they're not working. You notice and call his attention to it. You saw the problem, but he was unable to. Your action may have saved him a ticket or helped him to avoid an accident.

Sometimes a discussion between the Salesperson and the customer is sufficient to help the customer understand the problem and to take a decision to come to grips with that problem. Sometimes, however, the customer needs to have a vision created that illustrates the solution and identifies the problem.

A Vision Generation demonstration may be the mechanism for helping the customer understand the CBI that the customer needs to face, and a Solution offered by your products.

Vision Generation demos are another form of Generic Demo. The purpose is to educate and build a vision of a Solution in the customer's mind. There may be capabilities identified by the Selling Team that should to be demonstrated to create the desired vision and your Vision Generation demo needs to address these. Typically, these capabilities are the same or similar to the capabilities included in a Generic Demo. By definition, it may be difficult or impossible to perform adequate research to prepare, so making a Generic Demo may be the best choice for the purpose.

Generally, Vision Generation demos will be shorter and (even) more focused than Technical Proof demos, with smaller audiences. A good job with a Vision Generation demo may result in a follow-up meeting for a Technical Proof demo. A truly great job with a Vision Generation demo may result in a fast sale!

Trade Show Demos

I both love and hate doing demonstrations at trade shows. It is wonderful because of the opportunity to interact with so many customers. It is terrible when you consider how many of those customer interactions, and demos, are unqualified.

There are two major frustrating scenarios that often occur at trade shows. The first is when a customer walks up to a demo station and says, "Show me your product". The second is when a colleague in your booth brings a prospect by and says, "Show him/her our product".

They are really the same situation! Here's how you can improve the probability of success for these scenarios.

Hold back. Don't move the mouse, but hold it ready in your hand, as if you'll start any moment. Start asking questions, instead. Often you won't have much time, particularly if the prospect is not serious, but is just "kicking tires". Ask open-ended questions that lead the prospect to offer information on their situation, and their CBI's, and Reasons. (An open-ended question is one that cannot be answered with a simple yes or no answer). If you are successful, you may be able to uncover sufficient information to deliver a Great Demo!, albeit only if the Illustration and Specific Capabilities that you have available are a close match to the customer's situation.

What do you do if your customer is unwilling to provide much information or demands to see a demonstration before sharing any information?

The "Menu Approach" is an excellent solution for trade shows and similar challenging situations. It can be used for a range of Generic or otherwise unqualified customer situations.

Here is how it works:

Based on what little information you may have, which could conceivably be limited to industry, company, and job title, select and present the Situation Slide and Illustration that is most often of interest to similar job titles in the same industry. Then ask if this is what your prospect is interested in seeing.

If the answer is yes, then try to ask further qualification questions if the customer is more willing to share information. If necessary or as appropriate, continue with your demo, showing the Do It, the Do It Again, and Q & A.

If the answer is no, then try your second most likely Illustration, and test again.

You can present somewhere between 3-5 Situation Slides and accompanying Illustrations before either you or the customer determine that there simply isn't a good fit between your offering and the customer's needs. If that is the case, you simply close the discussion.

Axiom: *There are three likely outcomes when you share a Situation Slide and accompanying Illustration using the Menu Approach:*

1. *The prospect says, "I have that exact same problem…" You can then move forward into a deeper discussion and demo.*

2. *The prospect says, "I don't have that exact problem, but I do have something similar…" You can also move forward into a deeper discussion and possible demo.*

3. *The prospect says, "I don't have that problem." In which case you present the next item on the Menu.*

There is no sense in running through a full demonstration if the prospect is not interested! Presenting two or more Illustrations acts like a catalog or menu, increasing the likelihood that your prospect will see something that does address a CBI. You'll save yourself time, you'll save your prospect's time, and you'll increase the probably of a successful demo.

Note that you can typically present a Situation Slide and Illustration in two minutes or less—this means that you can easily explore 3-5 scenarios with a customer in ten minutes or less.

Now, what can we do about your colleagues in the booth that bring you an unqualified prospect? Train them! Teach them how to briefly qualify people, using the same processes we explored earlier. And then, teach them the "Handoff".

I hate football analogies, but this one fits very well. A poor or fumbled Handoff in a tradeshow booth results in no gain (it may even result in a loss!). A well-managed, coordinated Handoff can move you forward considerably.

A great Handoff consists of the booth colleague providing the following information to the person at a demonstration station:

- Introducing the prospect to the SE (at the demo station), and the SE to the prospect.

- Describing the prospect's general situation—the prospect's job function and main interests.

- Outlining the prospect's CBI's, Reasons and Specific Capabilities needed. Clearly, this may be a very limited set, based on the amount of time generally available at trade shows.

- Identifying any other important information. E.g., the prospect only has 15 minutes before he/she needs to attend a talk or presentation.

Prospects appreciate clean, professional Handoffs. It makes them realize that your company takes a real interest in their situation and in their problems. This opens them up and they will become more willing to share information with you. You can ask prospects to elaborate on the summary provided in the Handoff. You may even learn enough to deliver a truly Great Demo!—wouldn't that be a delight?!

Salespeople are naturally prepared to execute great Handoffs. It is your responsibility, however, to ensure that they are trained to get the qualification information and then to <u>provide it</u> in the Handoff. Often, booths are staffed with marketing personnel who should learn both how to qualify prospects and to perform professional Handoffs.

Note: There are a range of methods that can increase your success rate when engaging prospects at trade shows. Much of your success can depend on your opening question.

For example, you see a prospect looking into your booth and you walk up to engage him.

You say, "Can I help you?"

He says, "No." End of conversation!

Similarly, you ask, "Can I show you anything?" and he answers, "No, thanks." End-game again!

One simple strategy is to start with a relevant <u>open</u> question, such as, "What are you most interested in accomplishing at this conference?" This will typically cause a thoughtful response and provide you with useful information from which you can ask follow-on questions.

At trade shows where there is a range of vertical specializations within a market, you can ask, "What kind of [vertical specialization] do you do?" Again, this is a reasonable, meaningful question for the prospect and the answer will provide you with the ability to engage and qualify further.

Large Groups, Largely Unqualified

What if you were invited to give a demonstration, and although you were led to believe that the meeting would include the two or three people you had already met with and qualified, many more actually participated? What should you do?

This "expansion" of the size and variety of job titles in the audience at demos given at customer sites is very common. Many times it is an indication that your offerings have broader interest or importance than you may have expected—that's good. It is also good that so many people at your customer have decided to invest in the time to see your demo.

However, you have only qualified information on a handful of the audience that has appeared. What do you do? There are clearly too many people to qualify individually in detail, and they would rapidly run out of patience—they came to see a demo!

The "To Do List" is a very powerful tool for handling this situation. The To Do List method uncovers the major capabilities desired by a broad audience and provides a structured mechanism to address each capability.

If the audience isn't <u>too</u> large, perhaps up to about 40 people, you can start with your original Introduction. However, you expand it at the beginning. Ask each member of the audience to introduce themselves briefly by giving their name, identifying their job function and then by expressing what specifically they want to see in the demo. As they state their desired capabilities, you need to capture these capabilities on a whiteboard (or similar) as short sentence descriptions.

It is likely that there will be a lot of overlap in the capabilities the audience wants to see. You can use this to help prioritize these capabilities in importance, both for your audience and for yourself, by putting tally marks or simply incrementing the count for each capability as it is requested or re-requested.

At the end of this process you will have a prioritized To Do List of all of the capabilities your audience would like to see.

Your next step is to work through your list, verbally, indicating which capabilities your products provide, which capabilities you don't have, and which capabilities you will demonstrate during the meeting. This is a critical step!

Axiom: Bias the prioritization of your To Do List with respect to the needs and interests of your initial contacts and/or high-ranking audience members.

You should mark your To Do List accordingly. You can make two columns to the right of the list of capabilities—one for capabilities that your products provide and one for capabilities that you will demo. Placing check marks into the appropriate columns provides you and your audience with a clear understanding of the breadth of your offerings and the plan for the balance of the demonstration. At the same time, you should indicate which capabilities your offerings do not have, so that you set expectations clearly.

You can review the list, in your mind, and choose the order for demonstrating each capability. You may want to bias your list, and the order in which you demonstrate the capabilities on the list, to address the interests of key members of your audience. In addition, some capabilities may be linked and you may want to show those in one segment.

You can then walk through the To Do List, verbally, to let your audience know the plan for the demonstration. It is also important that you ask for agreement with your audience that the plan is acceptable.

Since it is unlikely that you have complete sets of data for each of the capabilities your audience wants to see, you may choose to use Generic Demos for each appropriate segment (capability or set of capabilities). If you have data from your research for any of the Specific Capabilities originally identified, you should use that data and execute those segments as you had initially planned.

Your entire demonstration, then, will consist of a series of individual demos, using either Generic or Great Demo! material. Remember to treat the To Do List just like a multiple-solution situation: after your Introduction, begin by showing the Illustrations for all of the individual Solutions—you want to set the "hook" for everyone present early in the demo and give them incentive to stay until their particular segment is unfolded.

As you complete each segment, and summarize for that segment, move to your To Do List and make a checkmark (✓) to indicate that the capability or capabilities in that segment has been completed.

When you have completed working through the entire To Do List, do a final summary that includes each item on the list that you demonstrated.

The To Do List is an extremely powerful technique for organizing and executing demonstrations.

Anecdote: *I was invited to present and demonstrate my company's offerings at a San Francisco Bay Area company a number of years ago. I had, prior to the meeting, discussed the objectives, CBI's, and Reasons of my hosts—two people. I expected the discussion and ensuing demonstration to be limited to these two people and perhaps one or two of their peers with the same or very similar problems.*

Imagine my surprise when I arrived to find a large classroom, which filled, over time, with over 30 people! How was I to manage this crowd of potentially broadly diverse needs and interests?

As I set up my computer, connected to a network connection, and adjusted the LCD projector, I asked people around me what their desires were for the demo—what did they want to accomplish? This gave me a general impression of what might be in store, generally.

Beginning, I thanked my hosts for the invitation to meet with them. Next, I confirmed the time allocation we had agreed upon—I had about one hour.

The next step was crucial: I methodically asked each person present to tell me who they were, what they did, and what specifically they hoped to see. As they listed their desires, one by one, I wrote them on a white board.

Many of their desires overlapped or were essentially the same. For these, I made tally marks next to the items. This showed where their interests and problems focused and provided me with the major CBI's and Reasons.

This process also helped me to link with the audience and establish rapport. More importantly, it also uncovered job titles that were particularly important for me to address or manage.

Most of their requests were items that I could address with the capabilities of my company's software. However, there were a few that I could not address—we simply did not have the capabilities they needed.

What I did next was to walk down each of the items on the To Do List, and identify whether I could offer capabilities that would address their needs or not. The items I planned to cover I marked with a circle-bullet "©. The items that I would not address I ~~lined out~~. I then carefully explained that our software provided capabilities to address the bulleted items, and not the lined-out items. I invited the people with bulleted items to stay, and those with lined-out items to leave if they wished. This showed respect for their time and honesty with our software's capabilities.

I demonstrated each bulleted item using the Great Demo! strategy, but without the Q & A. I asked that most questions be held until the end, in the interest of completing the items on the list.

Questions came up as I ran through the demo for each segment, in any case (of course!). Some I answered directly, particularly those Great Questions that led smoothly to the next point or to the next capability demo. Others I deferred to a Not Now List, written on another segment of the whiteboard. Some of these questions were answered in subsequent demo segments. In these cases, I drew a line through the question after first confirming that it had been adequately addressed—I confirmed this by asking the author of the question in each case. This then gave me the right to cross it off of the list.

At the end of each item's demo, I summarized and then put a check mark ✓ inside the circle bullet. As I walked down the list, it became very effective to see the items checked-off one by one.

Finally, after I finished the last item, I re-summarized. I walked back down the entire list, concisely reviewing each capability and making sure that I linked that capability back to the needs they had described. As I did this, I put another check mark at the end of the item on the white board. This emphasized the overall capabilities I had shown.

After this final summary, I thanked everyone for coming, and announced that I would then walk through the remaining questions on the whiteboard. Since the hour's time was up, I noted that this was the case, and offered that those people who were interested in the questions could stay and those that were satisfied could leave or stay if they wished.

Finally, I answered the remaining questions and re-summarized a final time for the remaining people. A couple of people then asked if they could "run some searches" with me. I agreed, and several of us spent the next 30 minutes working through some of their real problems. They were extremely excited to take away real data—real solutions—that morning.

The end of the story? I got the order shortly thereafter, and it was substantially larger than originally contemplated!

Product Roll-out Demos

When software companies release new products or major new versions of products, they may choose to hold an event to highlight and showcase these new products. These events often include a presentation with a demonstration of the new product. Audiences for these events can be large—from several dozens of people to a few hundred and up.

In these situations, it is virtually impossible to get to know much or anything about your audience. Your best bet is to use or create a Generic Demo that focuses on the capabilities that are the highlights of the new products.

A very important question to consider is, "what <u>are</u> the highlights of the new products—with respect to the business problems are customers face?" There is a strong tendency with new product roll-outs or new version roll-outs to focus on the new capabilities or features of the new offering. This is terrific—as long as these new capabilities are presented in terms of Solutions they enable or, better, real-life Critical Business Issues that they address.

If the new product has had the benefit of beta testing or early-adopter use, then your best move would be to execute a "Why did they buy?" study with these early customers. The information these customers can provide will be invaluable! It may mean being able to present real usage scenarios and Solutions as opposed to suppositional cases or, worse, lists of new features and capabilities.

You can establish some level of rapport with your audience by framing general questions with a request for a show of hands. This can provide you with some useful information as well as relax both the audience and yourself.

Exercise: Sign up to deliver a presentation or a demonstration at a conference or function where more than 40 people will be in attendance. Right at
the beginning of your talk, ask the audience to respond to a question that is
relevant to your topic or product, and that provides you with some good
information. For example,

"How many people here are already users of our software?"

"How many people are <u>not</u> users of our software today?"

"How many people didn't raise their hands...?"

You'd be surprised at how many people will raise their hands at this last
question! It is a terrific way to break the ice, poll the audience, and engage
them in your presentation.

Remote Demos

Remote Demos are demonstrations where the audience is physically
separated from the presenter. Most often this is accomplished using
"collaboration" software (e.g., WebEx, Live Meeting, etc.) over a network or internet connection.

Since Remote Demonstrations are becoming more prevalent it has
become increasingly important to understand how to make these
events as successful as possible. The next chapter is devoted to examining the pitfalls of Remote Demos and presents a range of solutions and
guidelines.

Canned Demos

Canned Demos are pre-prepared demonstrations that use the basic format of a Generic Demo, but are not run with the "live" software.
Canned Demos are inherently risky! This is because they are pre-

recorded, so you have no opportunity to make any changes or adjustments that may be desired by you or your audience.

Exercise: Using your web browser, go visit the web site of a software company whose tools you are interested in exploring. Locate and run their Canned Demo.

What is your impression of it? Did it "speak" to you or was it more of an undifferentiated "laundry list" of features (and presumed benefits)?

Now look at your company's web site and review your own Canned Demos—put yourself in the mind-set of being a customer. What do you think about your organization's Canned Demos?

Canned Demos may be used when a live demo is not possible. Additionally, many Canned Demos are run by your audience without your presence—and hence, without your ability to diagnose and identify their CBI's and Reasons. This means that you stand a good chance of missing their critical needs and capabilities.

Notwithstanding the risk, you may want to prepare Canned Demos for a number of situations where a pre-prepared demo is considered necessary. Here are a few examples:

- Web site-based demo(s)
- CD-ROM—or DVD-based demos
- Demos for videos
- Demos for staff that can't demo
- Software that requires extensive hardware and/or network requirements, that may not be available where demonstrations take place

Your objective is to minimize the risk of the demo failing, without your presence. Let's examine each of the cases above and explore how you can improve your probability of success.

- Web site-based demo(s): The web is a terrific medium for guiding people to the information that is important to them. If you have the time and resources, or if your web presence is considered important, you should plan to create a range of demos that address specific business needs and demonstrate key capabilities. You can guide viewers to see specific demonstrations using a series of lead-in pages that describe customer CBI's, Reasons, and suggest Specific Capabilities for the scenarios you need to show.

Choice of media for web-based demos is also very important. Consider carefully your target audience's Web connection speed for anything that needs to be downloaded. Clearly, you have a range of options (as this is being written), including:

- HTML pages, with screen-shots and text describing your narrative. This option provides one of the fastest response times for Web viewers.

- HTML pages, with screen-shots, video and text or sound clips. This requires much more effort and coordination. Remember that anything you create and post on the Web will need to be updated as your audience(s) and product(s) evolve. A stale or out-of-date demo may be worse than no demo at all!

- "Flash" demos. These currently offer the richest set of capabilities—the highest level of "cool"—for recorded web-based demos.

- PowerPoint presentation(s) is another option. This generally requires downloading the PowerPoint file. Use of video and sound clips is also possible, but bear in mind your audience's expected download speeds and versions of PowerPoint, video and graphics displays, and sound capabilities.

- Camtasia, HyperCam, RealProducer or a similar tool is another option—in this case you are actually recording a live demo, with or without sound, for playback by your audience. Again beware of download file size and speeds. Often, these packages provide both "creation" software and "viewer" tools that can be distributed with your demos.

- CD-ROM—or DVD-based demos: The same list of items, above, is also appropriate for CD-ROM or DVD-based demos. You generally have more flexibility with your options, since CD-ROM's and DVD's can be distributed directly to your target audience, but you should still be aware of the hardware and software limitations of your audience's equipment. Again, you can choose to create a menu system with specific demos for specific CBI's, Reasons, and capabilities.

It is likely that you can include a very large set of demos on CD-ROM or DVD media, so you may have more options with respect to the physical size of your demo files than you might have for web-based demos.

- Demos for videos: Videos are often generated as promotional or explanatory tools, to explain a business, a product, or a service. Videos generally require that your demo be very tightly prepared to attract and hold your audience's attention. An eight-minute video can seem like a veeeerrry long time if it is boring or off mark!

The simplest video-style demo is a direct videotaping of you delivering a demo. This can have the advantage of offering human touch—your natural warmth, humor, and domain expertise can be reflected since it is recording your actual demo. Some very successful video demos have been generated by simply recording an actual customer demonstration. This also gives you the opportunity to include some real questions and answers and give the flavor of the real-time interaction between you and the audience.

Again, you need to be sure that the capabilities presented in your demo match the needs of your recipient audience.

An additional advantage of video-based demos is that pieces of a video can be used for demonstration fragments in other media or "repurposed" for training or other needs.

- Demos for staff that can't demo: In addition to the Dilbert Pointy-Haired-Boss scenarios, there are a number of logical scenarios where there could be a need for Canned Demos for staff members who can't run the software themselves:

  - New employees in sales or marketing

  - New or highly complex products

  - Canned Demos for management to run

  The same principles apply as in our other Canned Demos situations. The key is to ensure that, as much as possible, careful qualification of CBI's, Reasons, and capabilities takes place. You can then construct one or more specific, Canned Demos to match the situations that are needed. Any of the media above may be appropriate.

- Software that requires extensive hardware and/or network requirements that may not be available where demonstrations take place: These are situations where the infrastructure necessary to deliver a credible demo is only available in a limited number of locations, or where setting up the infrastructure is costly. Your solution again may to create a Canned Demo, mapped to meet the specific CBI's, reasons, and desired capabilities of your audience.

What should your demo look like? Experience suggests that your Canned Demo should include steps 1 and 2 of a complete demo situation, typically:

1. Present the Illustration—Summarize

2. Do It—Summarize

The objective, for most Canned Demos, is to get the audience interested enough to take action. You want to provide enough information to generate real interest, but still leave enough unexplored to intrigue your audience to seek more information.

You may choose to run through step three and even step four if the demo requires it—for example, where you are providing the demo to someone in your company who will run it in your absence. This can work particularly well if a person from your organization controls the presentation and can start and stop the Canned Demo appropriately, to match the specifics of the situation.

3. Do It Again—Summarize

4. Q & A.

In all cases remember to summarize, summarize, summarize. Since you won't be there in person, you must let your audience know what your capabilities provide. Your summary, after each segment, is critical to keep your audience aligned with your demo and on track.

A few additional comments are in order. First, the more you know about your audience's needs and your capabilities, the better targeted your Canned Demo will be. The corollary is that the less you know about your audience, the less reason there may be to spend the time and energy to create a Canned Demo.

Second, technologies are changing all of the time. The examples listed above are (were) relevant for 2005. It is possible that by the time you read this other tools and technologies are available that make the examples above laughable. Notwithstanding, the key to success is to map the capabilities you present to those needed by your audience—<u>always</u>!

Note: DemoGurus provides up-to-date information on recording tools, screen capture tools and other relevant packages on an "evergreen" basis. DemoGurus is available at <u>www.DemoGurus.com</u>.

What about a "call to action"? In live demonstration situations, you or a salesperson is present to guide the audience to take some specific, desired action such as a purchase (yay!), an evaluation, or another more detailed examination of your offering. You need to include this call to action in your summary and provide mechanisms for your audience to take the action that is appropriate for the media.

For example, a web-based demo may have a summary page that includes a link to complete a form asking for a salesperson to call. A CD-ROM, DVD or video-based demo may offer a URL and a telephone number for more information.

Finally, remember that whatever you distribute via the web or other publicly accessible media may also be accessed by your competition. You need to decide what information you provide to them, as well as to your originally targeted audience.

So, Canned Demos may be necessary and important for your business. Make sure that you control as many of the variables as possible—audience qualification, distribution and call to action/follow-up.

Scripted Demonstrations

There are a number of companies and, especially, government agencies that often demand that vendors follow a specific "script" when presenting demonstrations of vendor offerings. RFP's ("Request For Proposal") scenarios may also include scripted demonstration requirements. These scripted demos present a set of rather unique and interesting challenges for the sales team.

Scripted demos often require that a vendor follow a specific pathway in a demo, in accord with the specific instructions in the script: "First show this, then this, then this, then that…" To add complication, there may also be time constraints applied to the demonstration in addition to the script.

On the one hand, vendors know that many (or most!) customer-generated scripts do not match the realities of productive use scenarios. Certain scripts may, in fact, simply be a canonical listing of the features and functions the customer has decided they want to have in the product. This results in tension between the customer and the vendor. The vendor wishes to present a reasonable set of use scenarios, based on that vendor's experience and so that the scenario allows a reasonable match with the natural "flow" of the capabilities as implemented in the vendor's software.

Contrariwise, the customer wants to "level the playing field" and allow a head-to-head comparison of the capabilities between vendors' solutions. The customer may feel that a script enables a fair, 1-to-1 comparison to be made.

These competing forces result in significant tension between the customer and its potential vendors (often with a fair amount of moaning, whining, and gnashing of one's teeth on both sides!). What can be done to improve the quality of demonstrations in these situations while continuing to respect the customers' processes?

First, you <u>must</u> respect the customer's process. This is paramount! If you ignore or substantially subvert the customer's directions for a scripted demo, it is likely that you will be disqualified right away.

Your first step is to try to work with the customer to redevelop the script to better match the flow and implementation of your software. Frankly, this succeeds in very few cases—but it is certainly worth a try, as if the customer <u>does</u> agree to changes in the script you can bias that script to match that of a Great Demo!

What can you do, however, when the customer is adamant and insists upon the script as written? Here is one solution that has proven successful in a number of scripted demo situations: Use the "Introduction" time allocated to present the relevant Illustrations and, if time allows, "Do It" pathways.

Most scripted demos, as rigorous as they are, allow some fair amount of time to introduce your company (as a vendor) and related introduction-based information. By cutting the traditional "Corporate Overview" short, you may have time present a set of Situation Slides and Illustrations that address the real business objectives underlying the scripted demo the customer has requested. Presenting these Illustrations can turn a scripted demo into a more reasonable situation for both you and the customer—they may even find the novel "introduction" refreshing!

I have even heard of situations where the introduction time was sufficiently long to allow the vendor to present a <u>complete</u> set of crisply executed Situation Slides, Illustrations and "Do It" pathways. The "body" of these demos still respected the customers' processes and followed the scripts as religiously as possible. However, a very successful vision was created in the minds of these customers in the introduction—which resulted in winning the business in a number of cases!

Deployment Demos

Ever heard of "Shelf-ware"? That's what happens when a company sells 100 seats of its software to a customer, but the customer only rolls-out 25 seats to its user community. The remaining 75 seats sit on a virtual "shelf". The likelihood of a salesperson being able to sell more software to that customer is vanishingly close to zero.

Many CRM (Customer Relationship Management) software packages are suffering from this problem today. They were sold on the basis of the advantages they offer to senior management, but the user population (often salespeople) simply did not adopt and use the technology. The result is unused or, equally bad, un-deployed seats.

There are, typically, three main reasons for this kind of situation:

1. The vendor sold the customer a vision that is unfulfilled by the vendor's software.

    I can't offer help with this situation, frankly!

2. When the sales process was complete (signed agreement and purchase order in hand), the sales team moved on to the next customer and failed to communicate the Critical Business Issues, Reasons, and the Specific Capabilities the customer wanted to the training and implementation teams.

    Interestingly, this is <u>exactly</u> the kind of situation that CRM tools were built to address! The remedy is to ensure that the key customer information is communicated to the implementation team (training, consulting, customer service, etc.) <u>and</u> that the training is focused on these specific needs in particular.

3. The Training department delivers generalized "how-to" training without any regard for the specific needs of the customer.

This scenario happens all too often. The result can be disenchanted users, confused and frustrated users, and un-used software.

An interesting, related scenario is when the <u>customer's</u> internal training department similarly ignores the specific situations and needs of its internal customers. The result is the same: unused software and disenchanted users.

For situations (2) and (3), a simple solution is to apply the Great Demo! method to training and deployment efforts. While training is necessarily a "how-to" function, it can certainly begin with showing "what" good things the new software will do for the user populations. Just as in a sales demo, deployment demonstrations must show clear value to the user up-front, in order for the users to be willing to invest energy in learning more details of the software.

Post-sale deployment scenarios are key to enabling future sales into a customer and to generating happy reference stories. Focusing on ensuring that deployment and training-based demonstrations are effective and successful may be just as important as the demonstrations done to get the order in the first place.

11

Remote Demonstrations

There are numerous web-based "collaboration" tools today that offer the ability to deliver live demonstrations or presentations via the web (e.g., WebEx, Live Meeting, etc.). These tools provide the ability to serve and share live software demonstrations or PowerPoint presentations via web browsers, with voice and/or multi-media transmission included simultaneously. Collaboration tools have the potential for tremendous impact on development, sales, deployment and support of software, as they offer the advantage of enabling people in separate locations to see and discuss what is happening, dynamically, on one another's computer screens.

Webinars, webcasts and similar events are now becoming popular marketing tools. Remote Demos are also seeing increased usage. Some organizations are just experimenting with the medium, others use Remote Demos routinely.

Here's the challenge: in a Remote Demo, every communication must be accomplished via a network or internet connection and a telephone (or voice-over-IP). Imagine how hard it may be to transmit your personality, your presentation style, and your movements through a wire (or wireless) connection. Similarly, imagine trying to gauge your audience's reaction—when you can't see them!

Exercise: *Close your eyes. Can you see what I am doing?*

(I was reading email…!)

The name of the game in Remote Demonstrations is <u>interactivity</u>! Your ability to attract and compel your audience's attention is your recipe for success.

How many times have you been on the receiving end of a web-based (remote) demonstration and found your attention wandering? Worse, do you find yourself flipping over to read email, or muting your telephone speaker to talk with colleagues, or simply dropping out of the demonstration?

Now turn the picture around and imagine yourself giving a Remote Demonstration. Is your audience paying attention? Are you losing people? Are you achieving the objective of your demonstration?

Exercise: *Find a partner and go into a conference room—sit at opposite ends of the room, facing away from one another.*

Have both of you close your eyes.

Now, describe a recent particularly nice restaurant and meal to your partner.

Try to access their reaction—and ask your partner what they think about your description.

Now, re-seat yourselves across from one another and repeat the process, but with your eyes open. How is it different?

Remote Demonstrations are a doubly difficult challenge in the sale, marketing, and deployment of software. It is hard enough to create a compelling demonstration that addresses your customers' key interests without the added complexity of executing the demo over web and telephone connections.

Let's explore some methods to increase the probability of success with Remote Demos. To start, we'll examine a few pragmatic guidelines for when to use Remote Demos. Then, we can explore ideas for how to prepare before the demo and how to generate interactivity to compel your audience to pay rapt attention during the demonstration itself.

Best and Worst Practices

The good news is that Remote Demonstration tools and technology now offer the means to connect with your audience and demonstrate your offerings without stepping onto an airplane. This can greatly reduce the cost-of-sales as well as reduce the time otherwise lost on the road. These economics are greatest driving forces in executing Remote Demos as opposed to face-to-face meetings.

Additionally, the ability to schedule a Remote Demo in a few minutes means that you can react very rapidly to time-sensitive opportunities. A customer who says "We need to make our decision by tomorrow…" might previously have been lost to the competition. Now you have a fighting chance to make yourselves equal, if not better, well before the deadline.

Finally, Remote Demonstrations are a terrific vehicle for offering "delta" updates—presenting the key capabilities of a new release, for example, to a customer who has already been exposed to the product.

The bad news: pundits have offered that Remote Demonstrations are for "when you absolutely, positively want to <u>lose</u> the sale…!" While this statement seems harsh, there are larger risks in Remote Demonstrations than in face-to-face demos. The reasons are clear: there is little or no direct interaction with your audience. You lose the feedback you would otherwise receive from facial reactions, puzzled looks, and pending-but-unspoken questions. Customers are less likely to speak up and ask questions in a Remote Demo than in a face-to-face situation.

Everything else being equal, I strongly prefer face-to-face interactions with my customers rather than Remote Demonstrations. For critical sales projects or other important events, I recommend that you choose a face-to-face meeting over a Remote Demonstration.

In fact, my general preference is to deliver a demonstration in person whenever possible.

However, budgets, time, and people resources are finite, and so you may want or need to execute Remote Demonstrations to manage your time, workload, or budget constraints. Here is guidance on how to get the most out of the medium when you do need (or want) to use it.

When To Use Remote Demos

If you have important demonstration, but you are limited by time, budget, or other factors and need to use a Remote Demo, your best bet is to split your forces. While this may sound counter-intuitive (you are still sending one person to the customer's site), it still saves significant resources while enabling a very effective demonstration.

For example, your technical resource (SE) can remain at the headquarters and perform the demonstration remotely. However, you will be most effective when a representative is also present with the customer, so that he/she can assess the audience's reaction and monitor the pace. A key advantage of this approach is that the customer will also be compelled to pay attention, since the representative is there making sure it happens!

The next-best situation is when you <u>already</u> have a good working relationship with your audience. The respect and credibility that you have already earned buys their increased attention.

Finally, <u>one-on-one</u> situations are often manageable, since your audience cannot "hide" in the midst of other participants.

However, it is unrealistic to expect that you always either already know your customer well or can have a representative present for the demo. Let's explore how to improve your odds in any Remote Demo situation.

Generating <u>Interactivity</u> is Critical!

Since your audience cannot you and you cannot see them (web-cameras are an exception), you must find a way to "push" your personality, movements, and enthusiasm through the network and telephone connections. Similarly, you must "pull" the audiences responses and reactions back to you through the same media. Here are tools that can help to increase the connection between you and your audience:

- You can use "Outbound" tools to increase the level of interaction with your audience:

  - Toggle between a Demonstration Roadmap (e.g. in Power-Point) and your software to provide guidance, keep the audience on track, and break up the demonstration into easily consumable segments.

  - Use the "pen" or similar tools in PowerPoint or the collaboration software to underline, highlight and emphasize keep points. The act of a new graphic dynamically appearing wakes people up and draws their attention.

- "Bidirectional" tools offer even stronger links with your audience:

- For large audiences, use the "polling" tools in collaboration software to enable the audience to vote and express opinions. People are inherently curious to see how the results compare with their own ideas, and they will pay attention as a result.

- Here's a terrifically powerful tip: give control of your desktop to an audience volunteer and have the volunteer "drive" for a while. The volunteer naturally becomes intimately engaged, and the balance of the audience will be on the edge of their seats to see what will happen—will the volunteer make a mistake?

  This is a truly powerful technique. It has the added advantage of tacitly proving that your software is easy to use—"if the volunteer could do it, so could I…"

  If you are in a situation where you have a "Champion" in your audience, you may want to choose to have your Champion be the volunteer. Even better, arrange ahead of time with your champion and organize a brief rehearsal. This will eliminate most remaining risk while providing all of the advantages of having the volunteer run the software.

- Another strategy is to for you to ask questions verbally as you go along and make sure your audience members respond. For larger audiences you can pose questions that can be responded to using the "chat" capabilities.

- Encourage (continually!) your audience to ask questions, even if those questions end up on your "Not Now" list. You want to generate as much interaction as possible. When you do receive Good (or Stupid) Questions that you want to track on a Not Now List, you can open a Microsoft Word document and use it as the vehicle to capture questions. This is particularly effective, since your audience sees you typing the questions on the list—and when you do handle these questions in the Question and Answer section, you have the opportunity to change the font (e.g., strike-through is particularly effective!) to indicate when a question is closed.

Preparing Before the Demo

Here are simple steps you can implement ahead of time to improve your success rate:

- Check out customer firewalls, networks, and other infrastructure before-hand. Confirm that it works before the demo begins! Plan to do this at least a day before your demonstration, with your customer. Many collaboration tools now enable this to be done automatically.

- Spend sufficient time well before your demo to understand the capabilities offered in the collaboration tool you will be using. These may include various pointers, highlighters, marking mechanisms, sharing options, chat and whiteboard capabilities, and communications options. Your best bet is to set up a session with a colleague where both of you can experiment and become familiar with the capabilities available. You want be to ready to use them smoothly—they should be well integrated into your delivery.

- Set your screen resolution to the audience's lowest common denominator. Currently, many collaboration tools map your screen resolution downwards, which means that if you have a high resolution screen and your customer has a low resolution screen, they may only see the upper left-hand corner.

- Monitor performance on a separate "audience" machine in your office. This enables you to respond and adapt as you proceed. It can be <u>very</u> surprising to see the actual performance from the audience's perspective, compared to what you see on your machine.

- For improved audio quality, use a headset with a microphone. Speaker phones sound like you are talking in a tunnel. Even worse, your voice may drop out if you move your head to face away from the speaker.

- Before you begin, be sure to clean your desktop and your "File Open" windows. You may not want the customer to see your last meetings. It is amusing (but sad) to see Remote Demos that show where the vendor was last selling…!

- Consider dedicating a computer to Remote Demonstrations. That way, it will always be ready to go.

During the Demo

Once you are fully prepared, here are suggestions to improve interactivity and your success rate during your demo:

- Have your best, most compelling screen up and ready when you begin sharing your desktop. Start with the end in mind… Conversely, don't leave a logon or start-up screen up during a verbal introduction. Nothing bores an audience more while listening to an introduction than watching a blinking cursor in a "Login" box!

- Move your mouse slooooowwwly and deliberately. Remember, there is often a lag time between what you see and when your audience sees it. What appears to be a smooth motion on your machine may be ragged and uncomfortable to watch on the customer's machine. Software with sophisticated or complex graphics may exacerbate this problem (particularly when you are moving or rotating images or graphics). Remember that everything you are doing has to be sent over a network connection, and, generally through both your firewall and your customer's.

- Ask questions as you go. Do this even when person from your organization is present at the customer site. Don't assume the customer attendees are awake and paying attention. You can inject humor to help, such as threatening to "include it on the test" or similar....

- Here's an amusing one: resist the urge to point at your <u>own</u> screen with your finger...I've SEEN this! Shockingly, the customer can't see your hand...

- Finally, summarize early and often. The act of summarizing helps ensure that the audience is with you and provides them an opportunity to ask questions. You can use a Demonstration Roadmap to help give you structured opportunities to summarize.

The name of the game in Remote Demonstrations is <u>interactivity</u>. The better you engage, the higher your probability of success.

12
Style

Style is an important component for delivering Great Demos. Your style can improve your connection with the audience, enable mistakes to be forgiven, differentiate you from your competition, and be the foundation for a developing relationship with your customer.

Axiom: *Substance over style. Always.*

No amount of terrific style, presentation skills, humor, or polish can make up for a lack of substance. Your first objective is to clearly identify Critical Business Issues, Reasons, and Specific Capabilities, and to build your Great Demo! around the best way to show your Solution. Your personal style can support and enhance your presentation and increase the audience's willingness and ability to listen and understand.

Exercise: *Would you rather purchase a product from someone who is competent and whom you like and respect, or someone who may be competent, but who annoys or irritates you?*

Think about the last three demonstrations you have seen, from outside vendors (not from your company). Which SE's made you the most comfortable? Visualize and consider which SE's you would prefer to work with over time, in a long business relationship.

If two vendors were presenting exactly equivalent products, that offered the same set of capabilities, company history, "whole" product offering, etc.,—everything else being equal—how much would style and your perception of the Selling Teams' personalities influence your decision?

Here are a number of Great Demo! "elements of style". Style really doesn't have clear boundaries so this is certainly not an exhaustive list. The following items, however, do appear to have impact on the success, failure, and especially the <u>degree</u> of success or failure of a demonstration.

- Humor.

- Appearance.

- Language.

- Buzzwords.

- Pace.

- Presentation skills.

- Linear vs. non-linear presentation methods

- Letting your champion drive

- Confidence and poise.

- Mouse movements.

- Screen pointing.

- Using props.

- Recovering from bugs, mistakes and crashes.

Humor

The moral here is to be human. Humans enjoy humor and appreciate humor (well, most do, at any rate). While I don't necessarily subscribe to the old axiom of starting off a speech by telling a joke, I do see positive results from interjecting humor during a presentation or demo.

The safest humor is to poke fun at yourself. The next safest is to include the other members of your Selling Team in a joke (as the target of a joke). It is generally <u>not</u> a good idea to make fun of members of your audience. An exception is if you have a long and trusted relationship and there is good give and take. A great time for humor is when you have a crash, a bug, or other hardware or network problems.

Anecdote: At a conference, presenters were coming up at the close of the previous talk to connect their PC's to the projection system and have a microphone attached to their shirts or blouses. Inevitably, one person's PC froze when it was connected to the LCD projector. He calmly hit CTRL-ALT-DEL and rebooted. Knowing that the reboot would take a minute or two, he filled the gap with an appropriate joke:

"Three engineers are sitting in a car and the car won't start.

The first engineer, a mechanical engineer, gets out of the car, opens the hood, and examines the engine. He comes back and says, 'It looks like the problem is the distributor rotor. All we need to do is replace the bad rotor with a new one, and we should be able to get going right away.'

The second engineer, an electrical engineer, gets out of the car, locates the fuse box, closes the hood and returns. He says, 'I agree with your approach but disagree with your analysis of the problem. I think we have a bad fuse. All we need to do is find the bad fuse, replace it, and we should be able to get going right away.'

The third engineer is a software engineer. He stays in the car and says, 'No, you're both wrong. All we need to do is open the doors, get out of the car, get back into the car and close the doors. The car should start right up!'

The audience laughed, appreciating his poke at the idiosyncrasies of com-
puter software and hardware. By the time his joke was done, his computer
had re-booted and was ready to go. Very polished, very professional.

Appearance

Overall appearance is much more than one's clothing or grooming.
Appearance extends to your equipment, marketing materials, briefcase,
and everything you bring with you to a demonstration at a customer
site:

- Make sure than any information or materials you plan to leave
  with your customer is clean and unblemished.

- Your computer and other hardware need to be in good physical
  shape—clean the screen of your laptop before you get to the
  account!

- Rats nests are for rats—make sure that your cords and cabling is
  well-organized and ready for service.

- Prepare the meeting room, even if it isn't yours. If you have
  time before the demo (ask for it ahead of time!), organize the
  chairs and tables. Remove any debris that may have been left
  from previous meetings. Make sure that the whiteboard(s) are
  clean. Even if it is not your room, the degree of preparation of
  the room reflects on you and your demonstration.

If you are giving a demo at one of your own offices, the guidelines
above are even more important. Take ten minutes well before your customer is scheduled to arrive and make sure the room is prepared properly:

- Computer screens are clean.

- Cabling is orderly.

- Tables and chairs organized.

- Debris removed.

- Whiteboard(s) clean and ready.

- Coffee and other refreshments prepared.

- Corporate, marketing and technical literature prepared.

- Give-aways ready to go.

If you have the use of a secretary or assistant, work with him or her to create a Customer Meeting Preparation Sheet that focuses on ensuring that the infrastructure is all ready. You can include the items above, plus, for example:

- Flight and/or hotel arrangements for the visitors.

- Transportation for the visitors. (Taxi or limo to the airport? What time?)

- Directions to a restaurant for dinner.

- Secretary or assistant's contact information, in case of any travel problems.

What to wear? This is a tough area to make concrete recommendations. While I'd like to believe that a person's substance far outweighs appearance, in reality this is often not the case.

Your best bet is to try to match your level of dress to the norms of your market. Science and technology companies tend to be more comfortable with what is often referred to as "business casual". Finance and banking firms may have expectations of business suits as the only acceptable clothing.

There are certainly regional differences to take into account as well. In Japan today, for example, <u>everyone</u> in a professional role is expected to wear a business suit. In Silicon Valley, on the other hand, nearly any kind of clothing may acceptable, as long as it is clean!

In general, salespeople are expected to lean more towards business suits and SE's are expected to "look" more technical. You need to calibrate what you feel comfortable wearing against the market, the region, the specific customer, and whether it is your first visit or not. A safe standard is to start one "dress level" up from your standard for your first visit and then adjust for subsequent visits.

Often, customers will tell you how to dress for visits at their site. If they offer this information, respect it.

Language

I'm not talking about English vs. French vs. Ancient Greek (go ahead and give a demo in Ancient Greek if you can!). The issue here is style.

SE's, in particular, are perceived as technical people and are expected to be conversant with the appropriate terms for their marketplace, applications, and relevant software and database environments. As a SE, you need to be competent but <u>not</u> arrogant!

Here are suggestions that can help provide guidance:

- Map the technical level of your presentation to that of your audience. Talking above them (too much technical information or detail) may alienate them. Talking below them may jeopardize their perception of your competence. You can determine the appropriate level through your research work, when preparing for the demonstration.

- Minimize the use of acronyms. If your audience is clearly comfortable and knowledgeable of the acronyms you use, then you can go ahead and use them. If they are not, minimize their use and instead use the full words. One good "happy medium" is to state the full words initially, followed by the acronym. Do this three times in the course of the demo, and then you should be able to use the acronym thereafter.

- Word phrasing can be important. Even subtle changes in word phrasing can make a large difference in perceptions.

  - Consider using "I'd like to <u>share</u> with you how we…" vs. "I'll <u>show</u> you how we…"

  - Consider using "This will <u>enable</u> you to…" vs. "This will <u>allow</u> you to…" Similarly, consider "This <u>provides</u> you with the ability to…" vs. "This <u>lets</u> you…"

  - "I" vs. "We"—"We" is often received more favorably. For example, in a summary, compare, "This afternoon, <u>I showed</u> you several key capabilities…" vs. "This afternoon, <u>we explored</u> several key capabilities…"

  - "But" can be heard as "no". For example, "I understand what you are saying, but…." In this case "but" really means "no, I disagree". Be aware of this! One solution is to use "and" anytime you are inclined to say "but". Try it!

Ultimately, you need to be comfortable with your presentation and with your style. Your choice of words can be a key part of your personal style. A Selling Team or entire sales organization may want to adopt or use a certain style consciously.

Anecdote: The ex-Digital Equipment Corporation was so acronym rich that a number of acronyms were coined just to <u>handle</u> the growing number of acronyms. For example,

TLA = Three Letter Acronym

MLMNA = Multi-Level-Multi-Nested Acronym

Note that even the name of the company was used as an acronym—DEC!

The Content-Free Buzzword-Compliant Vocabulary List

"Our powerful software is flexible, intuitive, easy-to-use and integrates seamlessly with your other tools. Robust and scalable, your organization can enjoy the benefits of our best-of-breed world-class offering."

How many times have you read this in marketing materials for software or heard it in demonstration meetings? Does it provide you with any real information—or is it simply a string of meaningless buzzwords?

When you or your team uses these words and phrases in a presentation or software demonstration, you risk loss of credibility. Demos, in particular, need to focus on facts—not supposition—in order to achieve technical proof or generate a real vision in the customers' minds.

Customers do pay attention to the words you use. For example, in my management roles as a customer I would typically invest twenty minutes in an initial meeting with a vendor. If that vendor offered platitudes without specifics, I would offer that vendor the exit!

Salespeople and marketing teams that avoid buzzwords and use specific examples do enjoy greater success in their endeavors. Sales folks that focus on their customers' specific situations and CBI's are rewarded with crisper, more predictable sales. On the other hand, sales people who offer buzzwords and similar meaningless phrases tend to suffer longer sales cycles and consume more technical resources than their more focused colleagues.

In the same vein, marketing staff that provide concrete examples to their sales team and customers are much more often sought-out, utilized, and rewarded. Conversely, marketers who fill their customer interactions with buzzwords tend to be sidelined from future customer-related activities.

Here's the list of words that can get you and your team into trouble—I call it the "Content-Free Buzzword-Compliant Vocabulary List":

1. Robust
2. Powerful
3. Flexible
4. Integrated
5. Seamless
6. Extensible
7. Scalable
8. Interoperable
9. Easy-to-use
10. Intuitive
11. User-friendly
12. Comprehensive
13. Best-of-breed
14. World-class
15. Cutting-Edge

How can you communicate the ideas behind these buzzwords and stay in the land of facts? Look for concrete, fact-based examples that illustrate the ideas.

For example, instead of saying, "Our software is robust", you might state "This software is deployed and in day-by-day production use by over 10,000 users around the world today." Or, alternatively, try "Our users enjoy a 99.98% uptime on a 24/7/365 basis." The more specifics and numbers you can provide make these statements more credible and support your claim.

Similarly, you can replace the trite and hackneyed "user-friendly", "easy-to-use" and "intuitive" claims by being focused and sticking to the facts. You can cite the specific number of mouse clicks necessary to complete a task, for example. Or, perhaps you can reference that users of your software out-of-the-box have never found the need to purchase training. Just the facts, Ma'am…no hyperbole!

A good test you can apply to your own material is to ask the question, "In <u>whose</u> opinion?" If it is a quote from a customer, then that's terrific, and you should identify the quote accordingly. However, if the answer is that it came from your marketing department (or your lips!), then you should find a way to rephrase.

For example, if you find yourself using a phrase such as "Our powerful software…," then you should ask in <u>whose</u> opinion is it powerful? You can turn this from useless fluff to real stuff by providing a working example: "Our customers state that our software reduces their typical workflow cycle time from several days to less than an hour."

CRM (Customer Relationship Management) software has been a key topic of discussion in many organizations over the past few years. Nearly every CRM software vendor says their tools are "powerful". In whose opinion? Are they able to lift tons of steel or send satellites into orbit? What makes their software powerful?

Replacing items on the Content-Free Buzzword-Compliant Vocabulary List with substantive claims provides you the opportunity to differentiate from most competitors. Compare "Our powerful software is world-class…" with "Our software enables 10% increases in close rates, 14% reduction in sales cycles, and customers also report substantial increases in the quality of leads generated and pursued…"

Two of the worst offenders on the Content-Free Buzzword-Compliant Vocabulary list are "seamless" and "integrated". Everything, it seems, is "seamlessly integrated" with everything else. Why, then, is there so much work for companies that provide integration capabilities?!

Once again, providing real-life, fact-based examples is a solution that enables you and your team to rise above the competition and earn a positive reputation for being fact-based. "Our Sales Force Automation solution automatically enters all tasks, appointments, and telephone calls onto your Outlook calendar, without requiring a single mouse-click. Set it up once from the Preferences Menu and our software keeps all of your calendar operations synced and up-to-date with Outlook." Much better!

"Scalable" is easy to improve upon. With regards to the number of users, how about: "Implementations of our software range from single users in sole-proprietorships to over 2,500 users in Forture-500 companies." If you are referring to concurrency, consider something like "Our ASP installation is currently supporting companies with a handful of daily transactions to organizations that are processing well beyond 10,000 transactions every hour."

When a vendor says their software is "flexible", are they talking about software capabilities, or their willingness to be flexible with their licensing policy or pricing? Use specific examples that are focused and relevant to the customer at hand, whenever possible. Using verifiable, real-life statements will encourage your customers to respond with a more positive, open attitude—which will help you in achieving your objectives.

Stick with the facts, avoid meaningless buzzwords, and enjoy increased success with your demonstrations!

Pace

The pace, or rate of delivery, is a key component of style. Do you speak rapidly, typically, or are you more deliberate with your delivery? You may want to adjust according to the needs of your audience.

If you are doing demos in the U.S., for U.S. customers, you may find that there are regional differences in the rate of speech. Traditionally, New Yorkers expect a more rapid rate of speech than their colleagues in Texas. Be aware of the differences. You can either choose to modulate your delivery to try to match regional differences or you may choose to be different, specifically to differentiate. Pace is a tool.

The only real rules regarding pace are:

1. If your audience falls behind, you have failed.

2. If you bore your audience by speaking too slowly, you have failed.

You should be sensitive and careful when giving demonstrations to foreign clients or to other non-native English speakers (or whatever your native language is…). Assuming that the demo is in English, if your audience includes members whose English is halting or incomplete then consider the following suggestions:

- Slow down!

- Use shorter, crisper sentences.

- Choose simpler words over more complex words, whenever possible.

- Take time to consider how best, and most clearly, to organize your sentences and ideas.

- Avoid colloquialisms!

This last point is very important. Americans, in particular, are heavy users of colloquialisms. Most people use colloquialisms, analogies, and metaphors almost without thinking. Many non-native English speakers will have <u>no</u> idea what a barn-bustin', over-the-top, blow-the-lid-off, knock-your-socks-off thing is. And they might express some serious concern when you express that you want to "pick their brains".

Presentation skills

There are a broad range of skills and techniques that can be learned that will improve the quality of your presentations. I recommend enrolling in a course that focuses on effective presentations. Especially useful are courses that include videotaping you in one or more presentation segments. This is both extremely useful and potentially very humbling! You may be surprised at how you look and act—especially in relation to how you <u>perceive</u> yourself.

Such a course will teach you presentation skills including managing eye contact with your audience, movement, animation, and verbal dynamics (the use of contrasting loud and soft speaking volume levels).

Here are a few ideas that will help if you have not yet had the opportunity to participate in a presentation skills class or course:

- Speak to the audience, not to your computer screen and not to a projector screen. Try to make eye contact with everyone in the audience at one point or another—speak to that person, exclusively, for five to ten seconds. You'll find that they will nod their head to show they are listening, when you are looking at them. Once you've connected for a few seconds, move on to another person elsewhere in the room.

- Move. If you are at a keyboard, try to find a reason to get up, occasionally. Get out of your seat and move towards the audience while presenting an introduction or summary, for example. Return to your seat to proceed with the demo.

- When presenting at a whiteboard or projector screen, move yourself and use your arms. People tend to respond to motion. Don't overdo it, however. Make your motions deliberate. Use motion to underscore key points, or to show clearly where you are on a Roadmap, To Do List, or Not Now List.

- Dynamics—the loudness or softness of your voice—can be extremely effective in highlighting key points. People tend to grow bored with a constant volume. You can surprise and underscore a particular point by moving towards your audience and suddenly speaking more quietly. They will lean forward and pay keener attention.

- You can use bullets, check marks, or draw lines through items to indicate closure. This is very useful for longer, more complicated demos where you are showing a large number of Specific Capabilities. Listing these "live" on a whiteboard and then placing a checkmark (✓) next to each item as you complete demonstrating it is very effective. You can do the same using PowerPoint to show a Demonstration Roadmap, using the dynamic drawing tool in Slide Show mode.

- Strong presentation skills can be especially important in managing and answering questions. For example, you should never move back from the audience as a question is being asked—this can look like you are uncomfortable and can't respond to the question. You should look directly at the person who is raising the question while you stand firm, then respond directly to the questioner, and then finally address the entire audience while summarizing. It is even better if you move a bit towards the person who is introducing the question, as it is being asked. This shows your interest in their query.

- If (and when) you are using PowerPoint, try out the keyboard "B" and "W" keys in "Slideshow" mode. These keys act as toggles: In Slideshow mode the "B" key toggles between the presentation and a blank (black) screen; the "W" key toggles between the presentation and a white screen. (It doesn't matter if you use upper or lower case—simply pressing the key executes the toggle). Using these keys provides you with the opportunity to direct attention to yourself (and away from the PowerPoint slides). This can help you to make critical points, move to a whiteboard for an *ad hoc* drawing or to develop a concept, or otherwise break up the standard PowerPoint slide-after-slide-after-slide presentation!

These few suggestions are only a starting point. Learning and practicing presentation skills is similar to performing with a musical instrument. Those with natural talent will improve with a good teacher and practice. Those with less natural talent can gain confidence and become very effective through training.

Linear vs. Non-Linear Presentation Methods

PowerPoint is a "linear" presentation tool, generally speaking. Most people who use PowerPoint start at the beginning of a presentation and advance, slide by slide, until they reach the end.

In the case of long presentations and boring content, this is often referred to by audiences as "death by PowerPoint"!

Whether or not you use PowerPoint, love it, hate it, or don't care; here are a few non-linear presentation methods to help enliven your presentations and increase the likelihood that your audience retains your message.

A great way to break up a PowerPoint presentation is to make periodic use of white-boards or flipcharts. These draw the audience's attention to new ideas and new areas of the room, serving to re-engage their attention. Use the B or W keys in PowerPoint to blank the screen when you move to a whiteboard or flipchart.

Using a whiteboard or flipchart offers additional possibilities and advantages:

- You are able to develop ideas <u>with</u> your audience. They see you creating material *de novo,* and thus it appears fresh. The audience has the opportunity to participate in developing the ideas, as well, which dramatically enhances their ability (and willingness!) to remember the information.

- Material on a whiteboard or flipchart is then <u>available</u> to return to, rapidly and easily, whenever you want to refer to it. It can remain in view for the duration of the meeting—and afterwards—which is particularly important for key ideas and concepts.

- It <u>wakes people up</u>. Moving to other parts of a room causes audience members to move their heads (and bodies, possibly) to follow you. Going to a whiteboard on the side or rear of a meeting room is a terrific way to inject new energy into the presentation.

- Another vehicle to use is Props. Tangible, physical, handle-able; interesting props both help to wake people up and provide reality to a topic that is generally rather virtual: software.

Here are a couple of excellent examples of when to consider using a whiteboard or flipchart:

1. When mapping out a customer's workflow. Here, the very best situation is when the <u>customer</u> picks up the pen and takes over the presentation, while you sit back at the table asking questions, guiding, and taking notes. Is the customer participating and involved, at this point? Yes, indeed!

2. When developing your software's architectural diagram(s). Showing an image with colored boxes and lines in PowerPoint is <u>not</u> very interesting or compelling. However, when you develop the same diagram on a whiteboard, the audience sees the architecture appearing in a logical set of building blocks. They can participate by asking questions and being invited to map the architecture to their own environment. In addition, you can also consider including the same diagram in your PowerPoint slides, as a handout (paper or electronic), to ensure the customer has a clean copy.

Letting Your Champion Drive

"Stand away from the mouse and nobody will get hurt…!"

Most demonstrations are executed by an expert from the vendor—the "technical guy", "guru", "techie" or "expert" (I've even heard the term "demo dolly", which is certainly not politically correct…!). It is interesting to note that the audience is often comprised of end-users, who are decidedly <u>not</u> experts.

This creates a natural misalignment between the vendor's desire to generate a vision of "ease of use" and the customer's perception. The "Do It" pathway in a Great Demo! is designed to help build and support this vision of ease of use. Reducing the number of mouse clicks and moving the mouse deliberately can go a long way towards creating that vision, but you are still at risk.

Here's a better way to prove "ease of use": have a <u>customer</u> representative run the demo.

When a customer drives the demo, or at least part of it, two key advantages are gained:

- First, the balance of the audience sees first-hand that a non-expert can actually run the software and get to the desired end-point or output (without crashing, running into dead-ends, or other problems). This provides the audience with a <u>stronger</u> sense of proof of the Specific Capabilities than when the vendor drives. The sense of reality is deeper; there is less perceived risk of "smoke and mirrors".

- Second, the audience begins to feel that <u>they</u> can run the software, themselves. "If Bob can do it, then certainly I can as well…" This also reduces the risk of the demo appearing to be too complex or complicated.

An additional advantage may be realized as well: the demo event becomes <u>remarkable</u>. When your customer representative "drives", it is generally considered unusual. This can cause folks afterwards to talk about the demo with others, "You should have seen the demo today.

Bob drove and it was really cool!" The result can be a very positive word-of-mouth effect that ripples through the customer's organization.

A few pragmatic guidelines:

Work with your Champion or "volunteer" ahead of time. If possible, coordinate with your customer Champion, if you have one, or other lead user before the demo. You want to make sure the Champion is comfortable, knows what to do and how to do it reasonably well. You may want to set up a remote session to practice.

As a further note, if your Champion is really a Champion, he or she will typically be very willing to invest in the effort to "get it right". Why? Because your Champion has a significant emotional and/or business reason for the demo to go well. Additionally, involving your Champion in driving the demo increases his or her ownership in the overall process—and this effect becomes a positive feedback loop (the more involved, the more ownership; the more ownership, the more involved).

You may want to limit your customer involvement to the "Do It" pathway. The longer the segment, the greater is the risk of the customer representative making a mistake.

Finally, in the case where you do not have a Champion available, you can still contemplate using an audience volunteer. You will have to give greater guidance on the individual steps, but the effect will still be very positive. Another, more controlling way to accomplish this is to ask the audience, while you drive, "What would be my next step?" or "Where should I click to...?" This provides you the ability to manage the process and reduce the risk of things going wrong, but it also reduces the positive impact of a volunteer stepping up to the mouse.

The moral: it is good when you prove your capabilities; it is great when your customer does it!

Confidence And Poise

How do you gain confidence and poise? You either have a natural dose of confidence and have tapped into it, or you practice until you become confident. This book provides tools to increase your confidence, by understanding exactly <u>what</u> needs to be demonstrated and by providing a template for <u>how</u> to organize your demonstrations. This knowledge also builds confidence.

Customers respond well to presenters and demonstrators who show confidence—confidence in their skills, in their products, and in their company. This reflects positively on your customers' perception of you, your products, and your company.

Customers who perceive confidence will be more forgiving of crashes, bugs, and other twists of demo fate. They'll simply grant you more latitude.

The converse is also true. A visibly nervous SE attracts torment. There are often members in a customer audience who would love to hound, torture and generally prove the SE wrong or incompetent. A SE who exudes confidence tends to neutralize or even shut down these tormentors. Effective management of a potential tormentor's questions provides a powerful tool to increase your confidence and prove your competence.

Mouse Movements

The mouse is a powerful presentation tool. It has the potential to organize, detail, and guide an audience. It also has the potential to confuse or annoy an audience as well!

When you are demonstrating your software live, your audience is looking at the your computer's screen, or they are viewing your computer's screen via an LCD projector or similar device. That's all they see—the screen.

Your mouse is <u>you</u> when you present. Make its motions reflect your statements, explanations, and your overall message. You can point with the mouse. Underscore items, highlight items, circle, link and combine items.

Make your mouse movements deliberate and purposeful. Avoid any random movements—they will only be distracting. When you get up from the keyboard, leave the mouse pointing at the item you are discussing, or at the most important part of the screen. It is a natural and powerful directing device!

It is likely that you know your software products very, very well. You know where all of the commands are on the screen and anticipate them. Because of this, you are able to move your mouse <u>much</u> faster than your audience can follow. Slow it down and make sure that every movement is clear and understood. This doesn't mean that you have to explain every mouse click, but it does mean that your audience needs to see what you do clearly. Moving too fast will make your audience confused and make your software appear too complex—"user hostile". Moving deliberately and concisely generates the impression that your software is logical and easy to use.

Screen Pointing

There are a range of options you can use to point and direct in your demonstrations and presentations. The mouse is one of several possible pointing tools. When you are at your keyboard, your mouse is most likely your best pointer.

For many situations, a laser pointer may be available, for example at conferences or in large presentation rooms or halls. Whenever possible, I prefer to use a mouse over a laser pointer. However, in large rooms or halls, a laser pointer may be your best choice for working with overheads or other non-computer media.

One of the key reasons I dislike laser pointers is that they are very precise—they reflect every tiny movement of your hand. If you are nervous or jittery, the laser pointer acts like an amplifier. One millimeter of movement in your hand shows up on the conference screen as a shake a half a meter long! If you <u>are</u> nervous, try using two hands to direct, and steady, the laser pointer. Leave it on sufficiently long to make your point. Move it deliberately and even more carefully than a mouse. Don't flash it on and off rapidly—this will confuse and distract the audience.

Another option is to use a stick pointer. In a small—or medium-sized room a stick pointer may be a better solution than a laser pointer. Stick pointers naturally damp jagged movements, providing the possibility of elegance in your presentation. It also has the advantage of not requiring a darkened room. The major disadvantage of a stick pointer is that many people tend to hold on to the pointer too long or swing and play with the pointer for no purpose. The best strategy is to pick it up, use it to highlight, detail or direct attention, and then put it back down in a convenient location, ready for its next use.

One final option is your hands. Frankly, your hands are terrific pointers. They can point, surround, underline, move, guide, direct and generally form any shape you might desire for any part of your presentation. Take a moment and consider the flexibility your hands, and arms, offer for presentations.

The same principles should be kept in mind when using your hands as when using your mouse. Make your movements count. Move deliberately and confidently.

Using Props

Props are terrific. They illustrate, they provide reality and tangibility. Using good props can provide strong support to key points or concepts. They also help to keep an audience awake and interested.

Exercise: At your company, organize and deliver a twenty-minute talk on a topic to one half of an audience. Note their level of interest and enthusiasm.

Now do that same talk again, except include passing relevant (and interesting!) props around the audience during your talk. Note their interest and enthusiasm, and compare.

You can use props to illustrate problems particularly well. Props can be used in front of the audience, or shown and passed around, or both.

Many software companies don't think about the possibility of using props—after all, they are selling software. Be creative! Use props to help differentiate your company from competition, your Great Demo! from your competitor's standard demo.

Anecdote: A terrific prop was used by Uli Heigl, a SE at a chemistry software and database company. He began his demo by entering the meeting room, from the rear, carrying a large pile of books, papers, and reference materials. He brought these to a table at the front of the room, sat down and began to pore over them. As he did so, he sighed, and said, "I really hate having to look through each of these books to try to find the information I need. It takes way too long and I'm concerned that I may miss something. I wish there was a better way…"

He then looked up at the audience and said, "Hey, I wonder if this new software from _____ can do what they claim? I wonder if I can search for the information I need, right from my computer on my desktop, in a matter of seconds?!"

And then he did. It was way cool!

Exercise: For each of the products at your company, come up with at least one clever prop for each key application.

This is a wonderful exercise to run at a sales meeting or similar event. Amazing—it can be fun <u>and</u> productive at the same time!

Recovering From Bugs, Mistakes And Crashes

It is inevitable. No matter how strong your development organization or how well QC'ed your software is, you should still expect to find bugs. The best way to deal with bugs is to plan on them happening!

Axiom: All useful software has bugs.

Axiom: The pain and embarrassment potential for any bug appearing is directly proportional to the importance of the demo. Corollary: The severity of the bug that does appear is directly proportional to the importance of the demo.

If you encounter bugs when you are developing your demos, you may want to explore different pathways to showing the particular Specific Capability of interest. It may be that one pathway always causes the bug to appear (report it to development!). Choose another pathway, if you can. If the bug is directly associated with the Specific Capability, then you may have a serious problem on your hands. If the bug is minor, you may be able to demo and talk around it. If it is serious, you may need to have it addressed and resolved before the demonstration takes place. The only good news in this situation is that your bug may become elevated in priority, particularly if the demo is for a project of high importance to your company.

Alpha and Beta versions of software are often bug rich. This increases the risk of encountering an unexpected bug, even after you have identified a "safe" demo pathway that shows the Specific Capabilities adequately. Let your audience know up front that you are running an Alpha or Beta version. Tell them that you <u>expect</u> to see bugs—that is partly what these releases are for. Setting expectations ahead of time will reduce the impact if and when a bug does appear.

How do you handle a bug when one <u>does</u> surface, unexpectedly, in your demo? Let's explore what to do for cosmetic bugs, serious bugs, and crashes:

- Cosmetic bugs do not really impact the functionality, but rather effect what is seen on the screen. Cosmetic bugs include poor screen repainting, failure of a cursor to change properly, wrong colors or incorrect locations of certain features or commands.

  The best strategy with a cosmetic bug is to simply keep going and ignore it. It is possible or likely that your audience never saw the problem. You are much more knowledgeable about what your software is supposed to look like than your audience. If you don't tell them that you just had a bug, they may never know! With many cosmetic bugs, you can simply change screens momentarily and then change back to "clear" miscellaneous screen debris.

  Strategy: Ignore cosmetic bugs and continue smoothly.

- Serious bugs impact functionality so as to render it unusable. With some Alpha software, many features are simply not yet implemented and they cannot be shown. Other serious bugs include searches that don't execute properly or return incorrect results (that's a very bad one!), links that don't link, and automated procedures that return error messages.

Software is often unpredictable, but one thing you should <u>always</u> count on is that a serious bug <u>will</u> repeat in a demo! When you run into a serious bug, don't simply try repeating the segment verbatim. If you do, and the bug hits you again, all you have done is to prove to your audience two bad things:

1. You don't really know your software and

2. Your software really doesn't work.

Your best strategy is to:

1. Acknowledge that you ran into a bug. Make this a matter of fact statement, short and concise.

2. Describe what <u>should</u> have happened. Use your Illustration or other media (brochure, fact sheet, etc.) to show what it looks like, if possible. This at least offers some proof that the capability can work. This also may be an excellent time to use humor.

3. Pick up the demo at a point immediately <u>after</u> the bug, if at all possible, and continue.

This last point is very important. There is no use throwing yourself at a brick wall again and again (unless you enjoy that sort of thing) and slamming yourself into a bug repeatedly has about the same effect.

Axiom: *"Insanity is doing the same thing over and over again and expecting a different result."*
—Albert Einstein.

Get over it—literally. You may sacrifice proving that particular Specific Capability for the present, but moving ahead gives you the opportunity to prove all of the other Specific Capabilities you planned to address in your demo. You can decide later whether it is safe and appropriate to return to the "missed" Specific Capability to attempt to prove it later in the meeting.

One way to accomplish this is to complete the demo, without showing the failed Specific Capability, and turn the meeting over to your Salesperson. You can then decide if there is time and an opportunity to test-demo the offending Specific Capability, to yourself. If the situation with the software appears to have improved, you can make a decision whether to let your Salesperson know that another brief demo, for that Specific Capability, is in order.

Another option, if necessary, is to schedule a Remote Demo session to demonstrate the Specific Capability impacted by the bug or crash, after the session. This is an excellent use of Remote Demonstration technology.

- Crashes are simply no fun. A crash is, after all, a crash. Nevertheless, software <u>will</u> crash. The best strategy for handling a crash is similar to that for a serious bug, however, you are going to have to fill in for the time it takes to reboot the computer, restart your application(s), and move forward to the appropriate portion of the demo.

  In a Selling Team situation, the best solution is for the Salesperson or other team member to take the lead and direct the audience's attention away from the computer. They can go back to a PowerPoint presentation, summarize, describe the current location on the Roadmap, or even tell a joke.

  One excellent strategy is to use the time to begin to address short questions on the Not Now List. This also can effectively direct the audience's attention away from the afflicted computer or equipment.

The SE, at the same time, should blank the projection device, as possible, so as to avoid having the audience distracted by watching the boot sequence for the computer. The SE should work quietly and bring the computer, network, etc. back to order. Once confirmed that he or she is ready, the SE should indicate this to the Salesperson or whoever is filling in. When this Hand-off process is managed professionally like this, even a crash can be turned into a positive.

In all cases of bugs or crashes, stay calm. Continue operating professionally. Even if you <u>are</u> sweating, don't let 'em see you sweat!

Note: When connecting to an LCD projector (or "beamer", as they are often known in Europe), <u>never</u> screw in the cable connecting your computer to the projector.

Why? In the case of a crash or serious bug you can quickly reach behind your computer and pull the connector out, effectively blanking the presentation screen.

This can be extremely important! You don't want to have your audience watching your machine re-boot when you or a colleague is trying to re-direct their attention elsewhere.

Anecdote: A Selling Team was giving an excellent presentation and demonstration at a customer's site. The team included the salesperson, a senior technical person, and a SE. The SE gave a terrific demo, a Great Demo!, and finished, leaving the most exciting screen on the computer.

The senior technical person opened and began the Q & A session, and was handling answers verbally. One new question was raised, which normally could be answered beautifully with a simple example using the software.

The senior technical person turned to the SE and asked the SE to show that capability.

The SE answered that, "The system is slow right now... Why don't we wait until afterwards?"

The senior technical person said, "Oh come on, let's go ahead and show that capability."

The SE said, with some strong emphasis, "The System is <u>really</u> slow right now..."

The senior technical person suddenly understood: the computer had crashed at the final screen! The SE was cool, calm, and confident. He had simply moved smoothly into his summary and the audience had no clue that there had been a crash or any problem!

Team Play

Remember that you are not alone, typically, in a demonstration meeting. Good communication between the members of the Selling Team is clearly important before the demonstration meeting takes place. Additionally, good communication <u>during</u> a demonstration meeting will also improve your likelihood for success.

When the Salesperson is presenting or speaking, the other members of the Selling Team need to both listen to the Salesperson <u>and</u> listen, and watch, for customer verbal and visual responses. Information on the relative importance of various capabilities, Specific Capabilities, or other items can often be discerned by careful observation during a presentation. Similarly, when a SE is executing a demo, the balance of the Selling Team should observe and track the reactions of the audience. The Selling Team can also help to track questions, open issues, and make sure that these items are appropriately closed during the meeting.

How you choose to manage the flow of conversation and execute Handoffs from one member of the Selling Team to another is a matter of style. Using the added eyes and ears of the entire Selling Team is a pragmatic practice to follow when executing a Great Demo!

13

Managing Evaluations (For Fun and Profit)

Re-Introduction

This is supplementary material that many Great Demo! Workshop participants have found to be very useful. It is presented as a separate chapter, because while it appeals to both Technical and Salespeople, the ideas and recommendations may be more relevant to the Sales folks than to the Technical team members. Nevertheless, many SE's may find that reading this chapter will help to catapult their career into a sales role (so be careful…!).

It's your choice: you can read on, linearly, and explore what this chapter has to offer. Or, you can skip this material (for now…!) and jump to "Becoming A Demo Master".

Managing Evaluations—Introduction

There are, effectively, two possible forms of technical proof, as far as customers are concerned:

1. Demonstrations

2. Evaluations

Clearly, a demonstration is the less expensive form of proof. In fact, evaluations can be the single most expensive component of a sales cycle—for <u>both</u> the vendor and the customer. If a focused, compelling demonstration provides the proof the customer needs to see, then this is the best situation for all parties involved.

Notwithstanding, as customers wish to reduce overall risk, they may require an evaluation as part of their buying process. As with demonstrations, there are processes and tools that can be employed to increase the probability of success for software evaluations.

We'll explore a range of tools and strategies that help, including the following sub-topics:

- Why Do Evaluations?
- Successful Evaluations—key parameters for success.
- Evaluation Objectives.
- Purchasing Process—the way forward.
- Players and Roles.
- Sequence of Events.
- Pricing and Payment Terms.
- Observations and Tips.

Let's take a look…

Why Do Evaluations? Costs Considerations

Many vendors offer their prospects the opportunity to evaluate their software as a "standard" component of their sales process. When well-qualified and executed, evaluations have a good chance of succeeding and can lead to a completed sale.

However, in far too many cases, evaluations are offered needlessly or carelessly, or are poorly implemented and managed. In these cases, the vendor loses the sale <u>and</u> finds that they have also incurred a large "opportunity cost" for the use of the resources involved.

Software evaluations are expensive operations, for all parties involved. For the vendor, costs include:

- The Salesperson's time. This may <u>not</u> actually be a great deal of time—and this factor can contribute to the overall problem. Some salespeople will readily agree to an evaluation and the pass the implementation and management of the eval on to the pre-sales and sales-support staff.

- Sales Engineer time. This can be <u>very</u> extensive, depending on the specifics of the software and the evaluation. An important evaluation can consume a SE's time like few other things!

- Training. Many evaluations require the same level of training to take place as in a "real" sale.

- Consulting. Similarly, customization work may be required in order to run the evaluation effectively and/or to meet specific customer needs.

- Sales Management. Management may want (should, most likely!) to monitor the progress of ongoing evaluations and the associated resource commitments. Equally or more important, sales management should take the lead in deciding whether a specific evaluation should take place: is it sufficiently qualified, with clear objectives and metrics for success, a clear purchasing process forward, etc.

- Legal. Evaluations often require an executed license agreement, which may mean substantial a time investment from the legal group to draft and negotiate an acceptable agreement.

- Accounting. Similarly, depending on the specific terms of the eval ("paid" evaluations, for example), the accounting group is also involved.

Clearly, the effort invested by a vendor for a substantive evaluation is considerable—and potentially very expensive.

Exercise: *Based on the criteria above, calculate the costs to your organization for the last three evaluations in which you were involved. Now compare those costs with the actual revenues obtained.*

If you find the results of this exercise frightening, then you should definitely read on!

However, the costs are not borne exclusively by the vendor. The customer also invests a great deal of resource in an earnest evaluation effort:

- Fees. In the case of a "paid" evaluation, there are the associated licensing or use fees. There may also be fees for training, customization, or other services.

- Users. Representatives of the target user community are expected to invest their time and, in many cases, change their workflows or processes to accommodate an evaluation. In an earnest evaluation this time investment can be substantial—users will need to see positive payback(s) in order to feel that they can give a positive report at the end of the evaluation.

- Users' Management or Coordinating Staff. The key players that manage the evaluation process from the customer's side often find they are investing a great deal of time and energy. Often, the "Champion" is heavily involved and may have a large emotional stake in the process, in addition to his or her business objectives. A successful evaluation, purchase, and deployment may result in raises, promotions, or similar changes. A failed eval can mean the inverse…

- Customer IT Staff. For nearly all software requiring an installation at the customer's site, the customer's IT staff will be expected to invest significant time and energy. Most IT staff are not particularly happy about this prospect—they perceive themselves as <u>already</u> having more to do than they can complete. Evals just add to the pain…Clearly, anything that can be done to help their cause can result in better support and happier IT folks.

- Customer Legal and Accounting. The customer's counterparts to the vendor's legal and accounting staffs are similarly involved, and necessarily largely to the same degree.

Evaluations are not cheap—therefore, one should only enter into an evaluation for good reasons and have rational expectations for the outcome.

Why Do Evaluations? Customer Perspective

Customers and vendors often have different perspectives regarding why to engage in an evaluation. It is important to understand <u>both</u> perspectives to increase your probability of success for your evaluations.

For customers, there are a number of possibilities for why they might choose to pursue an evaluation:

- Deeper technical proof is desired or required. In this case, one or more demonstrations may have simply been insufficient for a customer to feel that technical proof has been completed. This may be due to a need to see one's own data or specific workflow used with the prospective software. It might be that the customer needs proof that its user community will accept and actually use the software (consider how many CRM (Customer Relationship Management) implementations have failed because of this…).

- References are unavailable or insufficient. Most "majority" buyers (see "Crossing the Chasm", by Geoffrey Moore, in the Reading List Appendix) need to communicate with references as a part of their buying process. For products moving into new market spaces or similar situations, there may be a lack of reference-able customers that are relevant to the buyer's specific situation. For new products, there may simply be a lack of references at all. Evaluations become a reasonable method of addressing a lack of suitable references, from a buyer's perspective.

- Minimizing or reducing risk. This is the overriding issue for nearly all customers who wish to engage in an evaluation. It is critically important for the vendor to understand which <u>specific</u> areas of risk the customer is concerned about. For example:

  - The risk of the software not been accepted, and used, by the target user community. An evaluation can confirm for the customer that their users can and will actually use the software as implemented.

  - IT infrastructure risks. For software that is installed at a customer's site, on the customer's computers and servers, an evaluation can confirm that the computing and network infrastructure is sufficient to support implementation and roll-out of the prospective software. Issues here can range from compatibility concerns with desktop computers and servers, to version and support issues with other required applications (e.g., Oracle), to network traffic and load. Additionally, the customer's IT group may want to understand exactly what resource commitment will be required on their behalf if a purchase of the software moves forward.

  - Performance risks. Closely related to the above, but often separate, are concerns about performance. This is especially true for customers exploring new architectures or where implementation means substantial increases in network traffic. For ASP or "hosted" models, there are often concerns regarding the performance of the application "going through" the organization's firewall. Performance concerns are tightly coupled to end-user acceptance risks and to overall costs of implementation. Finally, for implementations that are expected to grow from small starting points to large, broad-based deployments, the issue of scalability is also important.

- Risk of unproven capabilities. Evaluations are often desired or required by customers for whom "suspension of disbelief" is insufficient in a demo or reference. Examples include the need to use one's own data or workflow with the prospective software, to make sure that the software can truly handle the data or specifics of the customer's workflow and processes. Or, it may be that certain key specific capabilities are simply not demonstrable outside of a production environment, and an evaluation is the only viable way to prove the specific capability.

This list represents many, but certainly not all possible reasons why a customer may ask for an evaluation to take place. It is crucial for the vendor to gain a clear understanding of the specific reasons that drive a customer to request an evaluation. Similarly, it is equally important that the customer identify and understand its own situation and reasons for engaging in an evaluation. The truly professional Selling Team ensures that both the vendor and the customer elucidate and share this understanding.

Anecdote: There once was a salesperson who was so annoying that customers would actually agree to an evaluation if only the salesperson would then leave them alone. True story!

Note, however, that this strategy is <u>not</u> *recommended by the author... The salesperson in question was subsequently "moved on to pursue other interests".*

Why Do Evaluations? Vendor Perspective

Customers and vendors often have different perspectives regarding why and when to engage in an evaluation. Vendors often need to take into account the nature of their products and the competitive situation in addition to the customer's specific situation.

Vendors may want to engage a customer in an evaluation for a number of reasons or situations:

- Complex offerings. Vendors that have complex, situation-specific offerings that are best shown or proven *in situ*, at the customer's site, may consider an evaluation as a standard component of a managed sales process. Often, these vendors have found that an evaluation is inevitable for most customers and therefore include an eval as a regular step in their sales cycles and forecasting metrics. There are additional potential advantages to an evaluation that these vendors may also be trying to leverage (see below).

- Easy-to-implement products. For vendors whose software is simple to implement, with low implementation cost/effort for the vendor and the customer, may also choose to engage in evaluations as a standard part of their sales process. Many vendors of ASP or "hosted" software follow this practice. For them, it may be as easy to set up and run an evaluation as it is to deliver a demonstration (generally not true, but possible). Again, other potential advantages may be inherent in these evaluations that the vendor wishes to realize (see below, again).

- Engage before the competition does. Since evaluations often consume substantial time and human resources on the part of the customer, many customers will only engage in a single evaluation of competitive tools at a time. For some product categories, getting involved first with a customer, ahead of one's competitors, can mean winning the business almost by default. If the customer finds that the product they evaluate first meets the desired criteria, the competition may never get a chance to be tested at all. The customer may be unwilling to invest additional resource in another trial.

- "Once it's installed they'll never let it go..." Some products are so wonderfully compelling that once they are sampled by the user community, those users won't let the product go away. For a vendor, this is clearly a terrific position!

- "The customer wants an eval..." This one is rather obvious. However, it is important to consider and understand specifically why the customer wants to execute an evaluation (See "Why Do Evaluations? Customer Perspective", above).

For a vendor considering an evaluation of its offerings, understanding one's own motives and competitive situation are often as important as understanding the customer's objectives and desires.

Why Do Evaluations? When NOT To Do Evaluations

Since evaluations can be costly for all parties involved, vendors and customers should be clear about why they want to engage in an eval. Here are a few situations where one should not move forward with an evaluation:

- No clear Critical Business Issues (CBI's). A customer may simply express a desire to explore a vendor's product and request an evaluation to accomplish this. However, if the customer does not have a CBI or similar business objective they are trying to address, then the vendor should hold back from an evaluation—"No Pain, No Change". Without a business driving force, the likelihood of an evaluation progressing to a sale is very low.

- Customer wants an education. This is a similar situation to the above, but where the customer's purpose is clearly one of becoming informed, performing a comparison, or exploring new technologies, without any intent to purchase! Vendors should be <u>very</u> careful of these types of situations.

- Customer just wants to get the sales rep "off their back". Occasionally, a customer will agree to an evaluation just to get rid of a particularly pestering or aggressive salesperson. "If we do an eval will you go away…?" This is clearly a poor reason for an evaluation!

- Vendor <u>hopes</u> they'll buy…Often phrased as, "If we can just get in the door…" In the absence of clear CBI's or business objectives, this will most likely end up as a waste of time for everyone involved. Worse, a vendor that convinces a customer to invest in an evaluation for the wrong reasons will often generate a "burn victim", an angry customer. It may prove very tough to go back to that customer later on when real, substantive reasons to run an evaluation surface.

Axiom: *Hope is not a strategy!*

- No clear path to purchase. There are two requirements, typically, for a purchase to move forward: (1) Available budget and (2) Appropriate agreement by the key person or people in control of that budget. Even in the presence of suitable CBI's or similar business objectives, if there is a lack of support at the "sign-off" level or simply no budget available, then executing an evaluation will be a waste of resources. The person or people who control the funds need to be in agreement: if the evaluation meets the agreed-upon objectives then the purchase should go forward. If an evaluation is being used as a lever to try to convince a key person, then the sales process is at risk and the evaluation may be a wasted effort.

- Disagreement on objectives. There needs to be clear definition of and agreement on the objectives of the evaluation and the specific success criteria. An evaluation should not move forward until these critical parameters are delineated and both the vendor and the customer are in agreement as to what constitutes success.

Vendors should challenge themselves when considering an evaluation to make sure that they are entering into the evaluation for rational, well-founded reasons. "Hope" is not a good reason!

Exercise: Review the last several evaluations in which you were involved—and which failed to progress to a sale. As objectively as possible, try to determine the root cause for the failure of those evaluations.

Success Criteria For Evaluations

"Hope is not a strategy"—this is good advice and it is particularly appropriate when considering success criteria for software evaluations. Running an evaluation without clearly defined, achievable objectives is a "strategy of hope" and does not increase your odds of successful outcome.

Here are guidelines for organizing an evaluation to provide you with the best opportunities for closing the business:

1. Define and agree upon clear and achievable objectives.

2. Agree on the timeline.

3. Reach agreement on the players, their roles and their responsibilities.

4. Understand and reach agreement on the value equation.

5. Gain a clear, mutual understanding of the purchasing process.

Let's explore each of these in more depth.

Define And Agree Upon Clear And Achievable Objectives

An evaluation is generally implemented to enable a customer to manage certain risks. The specific risks and associated objectives need to be very clearly identified and measurable success criteria defined—and agreed upon by both the vendor and the customer. Optimally, the objectives should map to the customer's Critical Business Issues, Reasons, and the Specific Capabilities uncovered in Qualification and discovery discussions.

The more quantitative the measurements, the easier it will be to be objective in determining whether each specific criteria has been achieved. Qualitative measurements, such as "Did you like the software?" or "Do you feel it helped you in your day-to-day work?" can be difficult to assess accurately and put everyone involved at risk. Relying on such qualitative criteria can result in mismatched expectations and bad feelings at the end of an evaluation.

Here are a few examples of quantitative parameters and associated measurements:

Performance:

*   Time to complete a specific task (user task-based).

*   Time to paint the screen (network/application/server-based).

*   Time to execute defined queries and return results (ditto).

Ease-of-use:

- Number of clicks to complete a specific task.

- Time required to complete a specific task.

Handling of customer-specific data/formats or customization:

- Comparison against an agreed-upon output or format.

- Specific ability to implement an agreed-upon data structure.

- Specific ability to present or display agreed-upon forms, pick-lists, pull-downs, formatting, file-types, print-outs, reports, etc.

The best practice, for <u>both</u> the customer and the vendor, is to identify and reach agreement on the specific list of parameters, measurements, and associated success criteria <u>before</u> moving forward with an evaluation. If the vendor feels the success criteria are too difficult, then the vendor either needs to negotiate the criteria or withdraw from the evaluation. Similarly, if the customer is uncomfortable with the criteria being used to define the "Go/No Go" decisions, then the customer needs to negotiate until comfortable.

Both parties need to agree, ahead of time, before investing resources in the evaluation.

Agree On The Timeline

"Objectives must be achievable, measurable, and timely"—in other words, you need to reach agreement with the customer on the time-frames for achieving each objective, in addition to the overall timeline for the evaluation.

These are two separate, but equally important parameters. The overall timeline for an evaluation may include items such as completing a legal agreement, sign-off, implementation, testing, and a summary meeting.

Each individual objective needs to have clearly defined and agreed-upon time boundaries as well.

Here's a simple example of an overall timeline (a Sequence of Events) that incorporates specific times for a handful of objectives:

Day 0:	Define evaluation objectives, timeline, players and roles; Go/No Go Decision
Day 2:	Draft evaluation agreement key terms
Day 7-9:	Draft, review agreement; execute agreement
Day 12:	Install software, perform administrator training
Day 13:	Perform data loading/migration
Day 14:	Perform user training
Day 15:	Begin Performance Criteria testing
Day 16:	End Performance Criteria testing; Go/No Go Decision
Day 18:	Begin Task 1 testing; Begin Task 2 testing; Begin Task 3 testing
Day 20:	End Task 1 testing
Day 21:	End Task 2 testing
Day 23:	End Task 3 testing
Day 24:	Prepare Summary Report
Day 25:	Evaluation Summary Meeting; Go/No Go Decision

Note, also, that there can be more than one "Go/No Go" decision-point in an evaluation. In the example above, if the performance of the system is inadequate, then the evaluation can be terminated without further investment of resources (or the issues addressed before moving forward).

Reach Agreement On The Players, Their Roles And Their Responsibilities

Each person involved in the evaluation needs to have clearly identified and defined responsibilities, on both sides (vendor and customer). Those people who will be involved in each of the activities shown above in the sample timeline need to understand their roles and the specific timing for their activities. To add to the complexity, and underscore the need to keep track, it is quite typical to "parallelize" tasks in the interest of achieving certain deadlines or desired time-frames (e.g., the end of the quarter!).

A good way to organize and manage this process is via a Sequence of Events.

Managing Evaluations—The "Sequence Of Events"

A "Sequence of Events" document is a simple, yet extremely valuable tool that helps increase the success rate for software evaluations. Very simply, it is a table that shows the key tasks or events, dates, and responsibilities, that is created and updated <u>mutually</u> by the vendor and the customer.

Here are typical columns that one might use to populate a Sequence of Events for a software evaluation:

- Task or Event: The item to be tracked.
- Track: The arena in which the task falls. This could be a Business Track (e.g., Salesperson), Legal Track (e.g., license agreement process), Technical/IT Track (e.g., installation), User Track (e.g., specific tests for performance or capabilities).
- Target Start Date: The date the item is scheduled to begin.
- Target End Date: The date the item is scheduled to be completed.

- Completion/Completed: Whether or not the item has been completed and the date it was completed. This often shows an item either as "Open" or lists the date completed. For some items, a simple check mark can be used.

- Responsibility: Designation of who has the specific responsibility to complete the task or event. This could include one or more vendor representatives, one or more customer representatives, or both. Note that fewer people sharing responsibility for any item is typically better!

- Go/No Go: This is a key item to include in a Sequence of Events. A "Go/No Go" is a decision-point whether to continue with the evaluation process or stop it. It is wise on the part of the vendor to include a few "Go No/Go" decisions that are readily achievable along the way towards the final "Go No/Go". Several smaller "yes" decisions can make a final "yes" easier to achieve.

Information listed in a Sequence of Events should be at a summary level—a handful of words at the most to identify an item. It is not a Gant chart, but can be used in a similar fashion. It <u>is</u> important to call out and "parallelize" tasks that can be run simultaneously. For example, a legal review of a license agreement can be ongoing during an assessment of computing and network infrastructure. Putting tasks in parallel can help to condense the overall time required for an evaluation.

A Sequence of Events document is created "mutually", although most typically the vendor provides the bulk of the effort in putting together the overall list of tasks and events. A simple strategy for a vendor is to lay out a Sequence of Events with proposed dates and then work with the customer representative(s) to add, delete or edit events, change dates, and assign customer responsibilities. (A classic "trick" is to include a non-logical date, such as end-user testing on a Sunday, to test that the customer actually reads and internalizes the document). Creating the document mutually helps the customer representative(s) take ownership of the document.

A good Sequence of Events shows all of the important events and tasks that need to take place for an evaluation. A truly <u>great</u> Sequence of Events carries the dates through early roll-out and implementation—past the decision date and end of the evaluation. This creates a vision that the vendor is truly interested in a successful implementation and not (only) merely a sale.

As a final comment, a Sequence of Events document can help organize and coordinate other sales-oriented functions, in addition to managing an evaluation. Many Salespeople will use a Sequence of Events to coordinate internally with the balance of their selling team and externally with the customer Champion.

An example Sequence of Events is provided in the Appendix. You are welcome to copy and modify it for your own use.

Exercise: Create a sequence of events for a hypothetical, but typical evaluation. You can use this as a template for your next real eval.

Understand And Reach Agreement On The Value Equation

Many evaluations are free, but shouldn't be. If there is an exchange of value, then this needs to be clearly identified and payment terms delineated. (More on this a bit later…)

Gain A Clear, Mutual Understanding Of The Purchasing Process:

Do not start an evaluation unless the way forward to a signed agreement is clear, pending achievement of the agreed-upon success criteria!

First, is there agreement that the process will proceed, pending achieving the evaluation objectives? Is it clear who will sign the agreement (or approve the purchase)? Will this person or will these people be available on the agreed-upon date? Note that business sign-offs and technical sign-offs may be separate people, and both may be required to proceed.

Are there any other players that need to sign-off before "final" sign-off takes place (other key technical team players, IT, legal)?

Oh, and by the way, is there budget available?

The highest probability for success in an evaluation, with the most rational use of resources, is achieved when these parameters are clearly identified, understand, and agreed upon by both the vendor and the customer.

Managing Evaluations—Pricing And Value

Should an evaluation be free? In the words of a famous orator, "It depends…"

Many vendors assume that they need to offer evaluations to customers without any compensation in return. While in some cases this may be the right approach, in many others it is absolutely wrong! Very simply, if there is real value to the customer, you should not give it away.

Where does value come from, in an evaluation?

- The customer can realize value from the intrinsic use of the software itself over the course of an evaluation. Value can come from direct or indirect time or cost savings, from displaced resources, or other real metrics. For example, in evaluations that include a vendor's searchable content, there is a reasonable expectation that users will find and get value from specific pieces of that content.

- Any effort that the vendor invests in training, consulting or customization, data preparation or migration, or similar services represents real value.

- The direct costs of the people on the vendor's side involved in the evaluation effort represent value—people are not free, in business!

- Similarly, the opportunity costs of the human resources deployed in an evaluation effort on the part of the vendor also represent value.

Does the customer see the value?

Great question! If yes, then the customer should be willing to pay for the value gained. The sales team may need to negotiate the specific relationship between the value gained by the customer and compensation, but <u>at minimum</u> the customer should be willing to agree that value has been realized.

In some cases, it may be acceptable for a vendor to define a value for an evaluation, and then <u>forgive</u> payment. Nevertheless, it is important that the customer understands and agrees on the value equation.

If the customer sees no value to be gained, then there is a serious disconnect and the sales team should re-qualify the purpose and need for the evaluation.

Think twice before giving an evaluation away for free…!

Managing Evaluations—Payment Options

Here are some guidelines and options to consider regarding putting a price on an evaluation. We'll explore a few payment and licensing ideas:

Unpaid Evaluations (Yecch!)

This is, frankly, the worst option for the vendor—and it may not be the best option for the customer as well. Why? When there is no monetary commitment on the customer's part in the evaluation—no "skin in the game"—there may be an equal lack of real interest and commitment.

Paying nothing for an evaluation can also generate the impression that there is no value in the evaluation or the vendor's software. This can make it difficult to recruit players within the customer and gain commitment for their time and energy. This is not a good position to be in!

Conversely, a paid evaluation increases the level of importance of the effort for all parties involved.

Paid Evaluations

In a "standard" evaluation, for many vendors, the customer is expected to pay for some or all of the value realized.

How much payment is reasonable? From the vendor's perspective, it is as much as the vendor can get! In the best circumstance, payment could be the actual license fees for the software (particularly in annual right-to-use models). Similarly, customers should be ready to buy upon successful completion of the evaluation.

Customers should be willing to pay for any services consumed, particularly if those services are needed for any vendors' implementation. Services might include:

- Training (administrator, end-user, developer...)
- Consulting or customization services
- Data preparation or migration services
- Installation services

Customers should be willing to pay for "fair-use". For example, one might pro-rate and charge for amount of time the customer is able to use the vendor's tool(s) productively. This is especially true for ASP models where there is little or no installation or data migration required. It is easy to calculate a fair-use based on time when the software is licensed on an annual-right-to-use basis or similar model.

Two final comments:

First, one can always put a price on an evaluation and then, subsequently, choose to waive the fee for a specific customer or specific situation. In this situation you have, at least, put a value on the evaluation and gained some amount of "emotional bank account" in the customer's mind.

Similarly, a vendor can also assign a price to an evaluation but offer a full or partial refund of the evaluation fee if the customer moves forward with a purchase.

Exercise: *If you are about to propose a free evaluation to a customer or a customer is just now requesting a free evaluation, consider calculating and asking for reasonable compensation for the eval.*

If you agree on a price, and subsequently receive payment, then calculate the difference between the evaluation payment received and the price of this book. Send the author the difference…

License Agreement Options

Getting software license agreements through a customer's legal process can be one of the slowest and most frustrating tasks of an evaluation. Most "standard" evaluations require two license agreements: one for the evaluation itself and a second agreement for a license if and when the evaluation is completed and successful. This sequential process can be very slow and puts the vendor at risk of missing key dates (e.g., end-of-quarter).

One option to consider is the use of a "Rollover" agreement. The advantage is that only a single agreement is needed for both the evaluation and the final license transactions. A "Rollover" agreement is structured to contain the terms and conditions both for the evaluation and the "standard" use license.

A Rollover agreement can be made "automatic". In other words, it can be written based on the assumption that the evaluation will move into a sale. If the customer takes no action, the agreement simply "rolls over" into a sale automatically. You gotta love these! If the customer does not want to proceed, as a result of a failed evaluation or other circumstance, they simply send a "No Go" letter to the vendor. Very simple, very easy.

In a second case, a Rollover agreement can be written such that the customer must send an "Acceptance" letter to the vendor to trigger the sale. Very simple again!

Comments, Observations and Tips

In spite of the best preparation, planning, and good agreement between customer and vendor, things happen…

Here are a number of situations one might typically encounter and corresponding recommendations on how to handle them. Again, you may want to explore the DemoGurus community website for more information and additional scenarios at www.DemoGurus.com.

"Installation/Data Migration Wasn't Complete…"

Don't begin an evaluation until both you (as the vendor) and the customer are ready. This includes making sure that your software is successfully installed (confirm it!) and any necessary data preparation or migration is complete and tested.

A partial or poor implementation simply increases the risk of a failed evaluation. End-of-quarter pressures on the part of the vendor are a typical cause for this situation. It would be better to start once everything is ready and either miss the end of the quarter date (gasp!) or work with the customer to see if other components of the evaluation can be brought forward, removed or truncated.

"The Training Wasn't Very Good..."

Very often, "standard" end-user training is delivered to the designated user population for an evaluation. If that "standard" training does not enable the users to execute the specific tasks needed to complete the objectives, then the training may actually do more harm than help.

Let's put this into perspective: How would you feel if you went through a full day of training and then found that very little of it was relevant, in terms of the work you'd been assigned to do for an evaluation? Most likely, you would be rather annoyed! You'd invested a day of your time, when you have <u>piles</u> of other work to do, without seeing that training pay-off for you in real use.

Evaluation training needs to be as focused and targeted as possible to achieve the desired objectives (Gosh—just like a demo!). "Standard" user training may <u>not</u> necessarily be the right choice! The training needs to cover whatever specific tasks and functions the customer's users will need for their role in the evaluation. Too little training on these key tasks and the users may be frustrated and uncomfortable when the time comes for them to test the software in the actual evaluation. Too much non-relevant training and they will become confused with too much information, and annoyed with the time investment for the training itself.

Who should deliver the training? The Sales Engineer? The Training Department? The best bet <u>may</u> be the SE or other member(s) of the Selling Team—since they understand the customer's Critical Business Issues, Reasons, and the Specific Capabilities needed. If an SE is tapped to deliver the training, then that SE must also have the skills to actually <u>deliver</u> training (clever organizations often cross-train their SE staff to provide them with basis training methods and skills).

If the Training Department is tasked to do the work, then there needs to be very good communication of the customer's situation, from the Selling Team to the trainer, <u>and</u> the training needs to be constructed to focus on the key tasks.

Finally, whoever does the training may need to expect to reinforce initial training with follow-up sessions—often known as "Tips and Tricks" sessions (more on these later)—to address questions and issues that arise in the course of the evaluation.

Training for evaluations needs to be just as focused and precise as the other components of the evaluation process.

"Nobody Is Using/Used Your Software…"

One of the worst situations a vendor can contemplate in an evaluation is when the customer's users are simply not using your software. The end result of the eval is most likely not going to be positive, for the vendor…!

Here are a handful of recommendations that can help avoid this issue—or to address it directly when it does occur during an evaluation, so that you have the opportunity to "rescue" the eval:

- Are the Critical Business Issues (CBI's), Reasons, and Specific Capabilities needed by the customer defined and clear? If not, this may be the problem right here!

- Was the user training focused on these? If not, consider doing a rapid, very focused round of training right away.

- Are the Objectives for the evaluation clearly defined and agreed upon? If they are not, then you may need to stop the eval and complete this critical step before investing any additional resource.

- Is there a Sequence of Events in place? If not, there may be confusion regarding who is supposed to be doing what and when… In particular, you should check to make sure that end-user tasks were clearly defined and assigned.

- SE's/Salespeople need to stay on top of the process. Most typically, the responsibility for driving end-users to use the software falls to SE's. Whoever is responsible (and someone from the vendor <u>needs</u> to be responsible for ensuring that the end-users invest the agreed-upon time to use the software) must stay in-touch with the user population and gently, but firmly, drive them forward. Use telephone calls, email, and face-to-face visits to help this process. You, as the vendor, need to both drive users and be available to answer questions, clarify procedures, and generally "hold users' hands" through their portion of the process.

- One particularly effective vehicle is to make use of "Tips and Tricks" sessions. These are excellent mechanisms to schedule time with the users, answer their questions, show them how to accomplish the necessary tasks, and generally build a positive relationship. See the "Becoming A Demo Master" chapter for more on setting-up and executing Tips and Tricks sessions.

When users run your software and find value in it, your odds for a successful conclusion to your evaluation are high. Conversely, if "nobody is using your software" then you may be in deep trouble (often referred to as "deep yogurt"!)—and you should take action, accordingly.

"Can We Have Another Month...?"

What do you do when your customer asks for more time in an evaluation? Your response should depend on understanding what is going on and why.

Are there rational reasons for extending the term of the evaluation? Were there missed dates or tasks that were not completed according to the Sequence of Events? Or is the customer simply seeking more time for other reasons?

Fundamentally, as a vendor you need to understand <u>why</u> the customer is requesting more time.

It may be that your customer really wants the software and desires to continue to use it while the license agreement and purchasing process complete. Contrariwise, it may be that your customer has decided <u>not</u> to purchase but is uncomfortable in giving you the bad news—asking for another month delays having to deliver that news.

Another factor to consider is fair value for use: if the customer wants another month, are they willing to pay the fair value for the use of your software? If not, then why not? In addition, remember that you may need to provide support, hands-on help, and other services and resources as long as the evaluation continues.

In summary, determine the reason for the extension request, evaluate the reason and determine what fair value should be assessed in return for continued use.

Axiom: *Parents worldwide have evolved a wonderful, patent response to similar questions from their children—the answer is, "Definitely maybe!"*

"All The Work Was Done In Last Few Days Of The Eval..."

One often hears, at the close of an evaluation, that "All of the work was done in the last few days of the three-month evaluation". This symptom is indicative of several possible problems that you can easily address:

- Vendors often offer a "standard" timeframe for an evaluation (e.g., three months), when neither the customer nor the vendor actually needs that length of time. The result is that users may wait until the last minute (or few days) to actually run their tasks and try the software. The solution? Map the length of the evaluation to what is <u>actually</u> needed (gosh!). A shorter timeframe is generally best for <u>both</u> parties.

- If users or other customer players are waiting until the end of the evaluation term to explore your software, check to see that you have a rational and agreed-upon Sequence of Events in place. You may either need to implement one or establish reasonable check-points (or "go/no go" decisions) along the way to help the customer's players stay on the timetable. Another tool to help engage users and keep them engaged is to hold "Tips and Tricks" sessions immediately before and/or after end-user tasks are scheduled to take place.

- Finally, the act of users waiting until the very end of the eval to run the software may also be indicative of poorly-understood user needs and Critical Business Issues: "No Pain, No Change". If there is no <u>compelling reason</u> for users to try your software, it is likely that they will put it off entirely or wait until the last moment to fulfill the tasks asked of them.

"We Want To Expand The Objectives..."

As some evaluations move towards their completion dates, customers will occasionally ask to expand the objectives or re-define the success criteria. This can be a serious problem for a vendor! It may be good news in a wrapper, or it may be an indication that the customer is looking for a way out.

The key, as in all objections or similar requests, is to gain an understanding of the customer's reasons and motives. The simple question, "why?" is very useful!

For example, the desire to expand the objectives for an evaluation may indicate an earnest desire for a successful completion on the part of the customer, in an effort to satisfy new groups of users or beneficiaries. Similarly, it may mean the customer has found other applications for your software (and hence will realize greater value from its use) and wants to explore before purchasing.

On the other hand, it may be that your customer is looking to create reasons for the evaluation to fail—and they may feel they can accomplish this by "raising the bar".

In the more positive scenarios, you should negotiate in accord with whatever changes in the objectives or success criteria are contemplated. More users, more time, or more applications may mean increases in your fees for the evaluation. This should certainly be true if you, as the vendor, need to increase your use of your resources.

In the case where new applications or groups of users are under discussion, one option to consider is to complete the existing evaluation and execute the license agreement, and <u>then</u> explore a second evaluation for the new users or applications. A similar, alternative path to consider is to enter into a "pilot" license, described a bit further below.

Regarding the more negative scenarios, you may need to be ready to stop the evaluation and proceed no further. Careful analysis and discussion with the customer needs to take place before agreeing to any changes in the objectives or success criteria of an evaluation.

"Can We Use The Software While We Wait For Legal...?"

You've set-up for an evaluation properly, run it well, and have achieved the agreed-upon objectives and success criteria. Now you are waiting/working on getting the final license agreement through legal and purchasing, and your customer asks, "Can we continue to use your software while we are waiting for our legal and purchasing departments to complete their processes?"

Congratulations—it looks like you have a successful evaluation on your hands when you hear something like this. However, a "yes" response by you may be the wrong answer at this point.

You may need to practice "tough love".

Simply put, if you say "yes" then what leverage will you have to move the legal and purchasing processes forward? Letting your customer use your software prior to the license and/or purchase agreements are in place removes any pressure you can apply.

Exercise: Interestingly, when you pull something away from a person they tend to want to hold onto it even harder.

Try it—hold a piece of paper out to a colleague and then gently pull it back. Your colleague will hold onto it more firmly, without even knowing what is on the paper! The more you pull back, the harder your colleague holds on.

This is a great exercise in human nature...

You can apply the same principle in wrapping-up your evaluations. Don't be afraid to uninstall the software and take it away from your customer while the balance of the purchasing process moves ahead. It may just help them accelerate their efforts to complete the license agreement and sign-off on the purchase.

"Sorry It Didn't Work Out..."

Even in the best of situations, with crisp organization and clear agreement of objectives and success criteria, some evaluations will fail. This is an opportunity to be professional and thorough—and to set the stage for a positive future outcome.

The first step for a vendor, once you have received the bad news that the customer has decided not to proceed with a purchase, is to find out <u>why</u>. Clearly, this is critical information. It may impact other evaluations ongoing or in the future—and it may provide a vehicle to return to this specific customer in the future, as well.

Depending on the nature of your evaluation, you will want to be as complete as possible with your assessment of why things did not succeed. You may need to poll users as well as your "Champion(s)", to get the necessary information.

In all cases it is truly critical to be objective and to encourage the customer staff members that you interview to be objective. What you want are facts—not opinions—as much as possible.

The next step is to clean up from the evaluation professionally and completely. Uninstall your software, if needed, from the customers' servers and <u>especially</u> from their end-users' machines. Return everything to the state it was before the evaluation began. You want to leave a very good last impression—and not sour grapes!

Pilots vs. Evaluations

When should you consider a pilot as opposed to an evaluation?

A "pilot" is an actual paid license of a vendor's software that generally addresses an initial user population or similar "starter" scenario. Pilot licenses may also include incentives offered on the part of a vendor for the customer to increase their license, at the close of a specific term.

Evaluations may be best when:

- Your software works well "out-of-the-box".

- Your software requires little or no customization.

- There is no or moderate data preparation or data migration required.

Pilot licenses may be best for software that requires substantial implementation effort or prolonged use before value is realized, or is being deployed in a "seeding model":

- Your software requires moderate to high levels of customization, data preparation or migration.

- There is a complex workflow involved that requires extensive training and/or changes to processes.

- Value is returned to the customer over a (longer) period of time.

- You wish to "seed" key users and generate support for larger licenses over time.

- Your software requires or relies on an "altruistic" model for information generation (e.g., knowledge management tools) and a pilot enables the database to be developed prior to bringing aboard a larger base of users.

When you do engage in a pilot license, keep in mind how important deployment demonstrations and training will be to expanding the license…!

The "Database Breakeven Point"

To close this chapter, here is a concept that applies well to evaluations—and to other aspects of sales and presales.

How long does it take before a newly installed database becomes useful? Corporate knowledge management systems, customer relationship management tools, sales-force automation tools, business information management platforms and related tools all depend on the usefulness of the content in the database in order to provide value to the customer.

How long will it take before value is realized? Are there mechanisms to speed up the process?

These are critical questions for many software companies and their customers. The time from licensing to pragmatic, day-to-day use of a database-based software package often depends on the amount and usefulness of the data being entered into the new database. A valuable concept to understand is the "Database Breakeven Point"—the point at which a growing database becomes truly useful.

Clearly, a freshly installed database is (most typically) empty—and the value of the database content is correspondingly zero (since there is nothing there!). As new, altruistic users enter content into the database, the value begins to grow.

A simple test one can apply to a growing database to gain a sense of its day-by-day utility is as follows: A user will ask himself, "What is the likelihood that I will find what I am looking for in the new database, *as opposed* to finding that information the way I always have before?"

When there is little data in the database, users know that it is likely a waste of their time to invest in searching the database, since the answers are probably not yet present. Instead, they will continue to seek and find the information they want using their old, established processes (which, while they may be inefficient, users perceive that at least they <u>work</u>).

As the database grows, the probability of finding relevant, useful answers to questions also increases. At some point in time, the probability of finding the desired information in the database is effectively equal to that of the traditional process—this is the "Database Breakeven Point"—and users will then consider it worthwhile to try the "new" software tool <u>first</u>.

How can you make this concept useful in your sales, marketing, and deployment efforts?

1. Set and manage expectations: As a vendor, you can use your experience with the growth of your database in other customer implementations to help new customers predict and manage their situations. Setting reasonable expectations for value realization and tangible payoffs for users can make the difference between a happy customer and one that is frustrated.

2. "Pre-fill the box": If you can provide your database pre-filled with some amount of useful, relevant content, then you will be able to accelerate the time it takes to reach the Database Breakeven Point. An example of this is to include publicly-available information in your database at the time of installation at a customer—they can then add their own proprietary information on an ongoing basis. (And yes, you may also be able to charge for the public data as catalogued and archived using your tools.) Another, similar approach is to partner with relevant 3rd parties who can similarly provide content that increases the time-zero value of your database.

3. "Collect and curate": Depending on the nature of the database and its intent, there may be substantial content existing in other forms or formats that can be loaded to fill the database faster. In the best cases, this effort can take the form of a database migration project from one or a few tools into your new repository. In other situations, relevant data and information

may be scattered in a range of formats and tools throughout the organization. If you leave the capture and archiving of this information to the customer, it may take a long time for them to begin the effort and even longer to move substantively closer to the Database Breakeven Point.

After all, it is likely that you, as the vendor, know the most about how best to find, capture, organize and store data and information in your tools. You may want to include appropriate services in your implementation plan (paid for by the customer, but of course!) that accelerate the process and move the customer towards Breakeven as rapidly as possible.

The Database Breakeven Point is an important tool to understand and to use to manage your progress with your customers. Very simply, the faster the box gets filled, the more likely you will have a reference-able account on your hands.

14

Becoming A Demo Master

Caveat

I strongly suggest that you practice creating and executing Great Demos for at least ten demo situations before you read this chapter. Why? Because you really need to become confident and consistent in your ability to build and deliver demonstrations, without adding additional complication.

Once you have presented a minimum of ten demos in live customer situations using the Great Demo! methods we've explored, <u>then</u> consider consuming this chapter.

Exercise: I mean it. Go Forth and Practice. Ten times.

Adults learn best by repetition. Adults learn best by repetition. Adults learn best by repetition...!

Once you have completed ten live demos using the techniques presented in the previous chapters, you will not only be ready for the additional ideas in this chapter, but you will have worked up a healthy appetite for this new information.

Come back when you are hungry...

Beyond The Basics

The Great Demo! strategy is an extremely powerful technique to match your demonstration to the needs of both the customer and the Selling Team. It optimizes the probability of success for the technical sale.

Now we will explore a few additional techniques and ideas that will help you to become a Demo Master!

Know Thy Software

The more you know about your software, the more likely you will be able to create Great Demo! outlines and the more prepared you'll be in answering questions. Yes, this is obvious. Nevertheless, many software packages are complex, and many companies offer a range of products that are often interrelated and interdependent.

As a Demo Master, you must invest time in exploring all possible aspects of the software you represent. Try everything! Test all of the functions. Find bugs that no one has found before. Create highly complex queries that push the limits of your software's ability to perform. Explore the breadth, length, and depth of the databases and information sources available via your software.

Exercises:

1. *Find out how your software performs on various machines—not just your own PC or laptop. Go try it on a slow, old machine and compare. Try it on a machine with a brand new operating system. Explore slow networks, fast networks and a range of configurations.*

2. *Try importing and exporting complex sets of data or images to and from other products. Pay attention to data "fidelity"—what data or*

formatting information is lost? Nothing stretches most software like trying to move data between applications.

3. *For extra credit, try importing and exporting complex sets of data or images to, between, and from your own product family, your competitors' product family, and any relevant third party products that your products integrate with.*

4. *For extra, extra credit, read the manual and/or help systems for your products and complementary products.*

The more you have experienced your products yourself, the better prepared you will be for new sets of user requirements, new desired Specific Capabilities, and new questions.

Axiom: Demos Never Seem To Get Shorter

Have you ever noticed that "traditional" demonstrations for existing software products never seem to get shorter?

Think about it for a moment: Each successive release of the software adds more and more features and capabilities. Most marketing groups that create product roll-out demos tend to focus on the new capabilities for each release—but also tend to <u>add</u> them to the already existing demo!

This means that with each release of the software, the demos get longer, and longer, and longer, and longer…

The result is often long, complicated demonstrations that take <u>forever</u> to get to the point! ("Wait! Wait! Don't go! I haven't gotten to the <u>really</u> cool stuff yet…!")

The moral: We need to discipline ourselves and remember to focus on our customers' CBI's when we create demos for new releases of existing prod-

ucts. While you certainly want to highlight the new capabilities, you need to test to make sure that the new capabilities are truly <u>relevant</u> for the targeted audiences.

Similarly, you need to review the old, existing demos and (perhaps rather brutally) trim them back in length or (much better) start fresh and only include the best, most relevant capabilities for the new release roll-out.

Know Thy Complementary Products

It is highly unlikely that your products are used by themselves to deliver Solutions. You'll need to know any other products that are also required for a Solution as well as you know your own offerings.

For example, is Excel used in many of your demos? Then learn and practice Excel until you are as familiar with Excel as you are with your own products. Why?

What if you prepared a demonstration that requires data from your application to be exported to Excel, followed by the generation of a sorted report in Excel. If you fail to perform the sort, and to show the format of the report desired by the customer, then you fail to complete proving your own product's capabilities—and the demo is a failure.

Perhaps you <u>assume</u> that your customer can extrapolate and visualize doing the sort and formatting in Excel by themselves. But what if they don't know how? Then the demo is a failure. You <u>must</u> show the completed deliverable, even if it is completed using a complementary product.

The moral here is that your customer needs and wants a Solution—and the products and services that comprise a Solution may come from both your company and other firms. Your ability to demonstrate the full Solution is critical to proving the overall set of Specific Capabilities needed.

Exercise: Make a list of the products that your software relies upon or integrates with, that you may expect to use in demonstrations. Be complete!

Now go learn those products as intimately as necessary.

Note: some of these products may be complex and require focused training, e.g. Oracle Database Administration. If you need to gain this knowledge you may need to send yourself to appropriate training courses.

Know Thy Competition

If you are in a market with one or more competent competitors, then you should seek to learn your competitions' products as completely as possible. The act of doing this will offer a number of advantages:

- You may find features and capabilities that you'd like your own products to offer—and sponsor them to your development organization.

- You may find weaknesses in your competitors' products—missing capabilities or poorly implemented capabilities.

- You may realize where <u>your</u> products have weaknesses or are missing capabilities.

- You will gain an understanding of how to migrate data from their applications to yours—this can be very important for smoothing the process of replacing a competitor's entrenched product with your own.

How you use this information is very important. Often, customers will ask you to comment about competitor's software. Here are some Golden Rules regarding discussing competitor's software products:

1. Don't do it.

Yes, that's correct. Even if you <u>know</u> of critical weaknesses missing capabilities, don't call them out directly. There is a better way!

Your best response, when asked to comment on a competitive product or company, is to say something to the effect, "Since I don't work for _____, I can't really comment on their offerings or their company. I <u>can</u> tell you about our products and our organization, however."

Axiom: *Today's competitor is tomorrow's partner.*

So, how <u>do</u> you take advantage of competitor's weaknesses? You can do this by diagnosing with a <u>bias</u> towards the capabilities that your products offer (and your competitors' products do not).

For example, when you are qualifying your prospect, you may find that they want a simple report to be created with a set of columns and rows. Their original vision may be that the final report is in the form of a Microsoft Word document, with a table.

You may realize that an Excel spreadsheet, with the same information, will provide your prospect with a much more flexible report—it can be sorted and analyzed more easily, and additional graphs can be created that help to visualize the results more clearly. Even better—you also know that your competitor's product has significant problems or weaknesses in exporting data to Excel.

You can ask, "Would it also be important or useful to be able to generate your reports in <u>either</u> Word or Excel? Word appears to satisfy your basic requirements, and Excel provides the additional ability to further analyze and graph your data."

If your prospect likes this additional capability, and decides that it is important, you have accomplished two objectives:

1. You have created the need for a Specific Capability that your product offers and that you can demonstrate.

2. You have raised a barrier to entry against your competition.

Note the use of the word, "also". This is a subtle method of introducing a new, previously un-requested capability without risking "feature-glut". If the customer is interested in the capability, then it may become a desired Specific Capability. On the other hand, if the customer says, "No, I'm not interested in that", then you can easily drop the topic and move on. Note, also, that you don't demonstrate the capability unless they are interested in it as a Specific Capability.

Delightful, isn't it? The beautiful aspect to this is that you never attacked your competition directly. Instead, you diagnosed with a bias towards your Solution.

Exercise: Make a table of the key capabilities for your flagship product. Place check marks where your product provides these capabilities (should be 100%, or know the reason why!). Now add columns for your top two or three competitors. Place check marks where your competitors' products provide the same key capabilities.

Note any gaps in your competitors' offerings and be prepared to exploit these in qualification discussions.

Exercise: Take the same table from the previous exercise, and add rows where your competition offers capabilities or advantages over your products.

Be prepared to address these weaknesses in discussions with your prospects. Develop work-arounds or alternate pathways as possible—and, if these dis-

advantages are important, drive their implementation with your development organization.

Exercise: *For extra credit, perform a "whole product" analysis. This is best done as a brainstorming exercise with your Selling Team and/or marketing organization. The objective is to identify <u>all</u> those components that make up the full product that your company offers.*

This is not just the list of capabilities in your software. The "whole product" is your set of capabilities in your software plus all of those services, support functions, futures, third party products, existing customers, etc. that may be important in making a decision to use your software. Here is a start:

- *List of key capabilities in your software*
- *Documentation—range of documentation available*
- *Training—range of training available, range of locations where training is delivered*
- *Consulting and professional services available*
- *Customer support—systems, expertise, hours, geography, language*
- *Language and other localization support for all of the above*
- *Reference customers—markets, geographies, applications*
- *Total customers*
- *Third party complementary products and services*
- *Sales force—experience, competence, geography*
- *SE organization*
- *Development organization*
- *Management*

- *Product roadmap(s) and definitions of upcoming releases*

All of these can play a role in gaining and keeping customers. All of these can be "rows" in your overall table of capabilities.

Know Thy Customers

The more you know about your customers' needs, environments, situations, and history, the better your Great Demos will become.

Here are three ideas to consider in your quest to increase your understanding of your customers:

1. A Good Idea: Work with your Customer Service Department or group to identify key customer issues and unmet needs.

2. A Better Idea: Take product training <u>with</u> your customers to understand their impressions and planned uses of your product(s), and to hear their feedback on implementation, capabilities, etc.

3. The Best Idea: Visit existing customers and have them demo <u>their</u> applications and uses of your product(s) (and/or competitive or complementary products) to understand <u>how</u> they are used and <u>what</u> they use them for.

Remember that any information offered by your customers may need to be considered confidential information. You need to be clear on what specific information, or data, you can share with other customers and what cannot be shared.

Users' Group Meetings are terrific opportunities to learn more about your customers. The smaller the group, typically, the more specific information is revealed. Break-out sessions, new product focus or discussion sessions, demo sessions, lunches and dinners are all excellent opportunities to listen, ask questions, and learn about your customers' needs and desires.

Teach Thy Customers

Hey, what's this? Am I suddenly in the Training organization? In a way, yes you are. Each time your customer sees your product demonstrated you are, in fact, delivering training. While formal product demonstrations, used in the sales process, are clearly focused on selling the product, you may find that in an ongoing relationship with a customer there becomes a blurring of sales and training.

The wonderful thing about "real" training is that customers often open up and express desires and needs that remain hidden when a Salesperson is present. You can, and should, tap into this—but <u>respect</u> the trust and honesty that is shared with you. Don't compromise the relationship by communicating or using information that you know you should not.

A terrific mechanism that offers excellent access to your existing customers is called a "Tips and Tricks" session. This is something halfway in between a demo and formal training. It is typically a 1-2 hour session, held at your customer's site with a handful of users, where you actually work real problems with them.

These sessions are <u>very</u> powerful when executed well. They provide your customer with highly targeted, high value *ad hoc* training on problems and methods that are important to them. A Tips and Tricks session provides you with extraordinary intimate contact with your customer users and many of their real problems and issues. It builds trust and builds a strong relationship between you and your customers.

Tips and Tricks sessions focus on the "<u>how</u>" and less on the "what". Users will want to know, "How do I attack this problem?" "How do I use this capability?" "Is there a way that I can…?"

Here are suggestions for setting-up and delivering a successful Tips and Tricks session:

- First, gain agreement from the Salesperson (and any others as needed) before you go ahead and organize the session. Typically, these sessions are provided *gratis*.

- Second, make sure that you are truly prepared—that you are very well versed with your software! Confidence is one thing; execution is another!

- Contact your customer to propose a Tips and Tricks session. Let them know that it is free and targeted at helping users get the most value and utility out of their investment. Tell them that this is an opportunity to sit with an expert (you) and work real problems at their site. Finally, make sure they understand that they should plan to bring "how to" questions and real problems to the session.

- Once the date and time are confirmed, make sure that it is honored. Canceling a Tips and Tricks session is very bad—it tells the customer that they are not important to you.

- Prepare two to four brief Great Demo! segments that show how to use some of the most useful and requested capabilities. You want to have these prepared ahead of time so that you can use them to kick-off the session, if needed. It is possible that people who attend, particularly if they have never participated in a Tips and Tricks session, will not realize that they are expected to bring problems to be solved.

- Begin the Tips and Tricks session by having everyone introduce themselves (unless you all already know one another). Then ask for questions or problems—you can organize these using the To Do List method. If people are reticent to propose problems, then you can use one or more of your pre-prepared mini-Great Demos to get things started.

These can be truly excellent sessions for both you and your customers. You really get the chance to see the real problems they want to address, which provides wonderful feedback and information for creating even better Great Demos, as well as providing your company with improved direction for development, consulting, training, and sales.

Know Thy Peers

If you are in an organization with two or more SE's, then you have a terrific source of Great Demo! feedstock available to you—you only have to ask!

SE "Demo Days" provide a means to share demo tools, information, and experiences with your closest peers in your organization. At your next sales meeting, plan to allocate several hours dedicated to presenting and sharing demonstrations. You'll want to structure these as follows:

- Coordinate such that several SE's agree to each present one demo.

- Plan on allocating 20 minutes for the demo itself plus an additional 10-20 minutes for discussion.

- Include time for a short introduction and more substantial time for discussion afterwards.

- Decide ahead of time whether to invite sales, marketing, and/or other players. You'll want to decide what your objectives are for the time—whether you are strictly interested in sharing information between SE's, or want a larger outcome that impacts sales, marketing, etc.

For example, if four SE's each agree to present a demo, you might schedule your Demo Day as follows:

8:00 AM	Introduction and Review of Objectives
8:20 AM	First Demo and Discussion
9:00 AM	Second Demo and Discussion
9:40 AM	Break
10:00 AM	Third Demo and Discussion
10:40 AM	Fourth Demo and Discussion
11:20 AM	Discussion of Illustrations, Data Sets and Other Tools and Information Needed
11:50 AM	Summary and Wrap-Up
12:00 Noon	Meeting Concludes

The comment regarding being clear on your objectives is very important. If you do this kind of Demo Day solely for and by a group of SE's, then you will be able to focus on the details of creating and delivering successful demos. On the other hand, you may want to educate sales and consulting regarding the availability of certain demos, and/or want their feedback. However, the larger the group, the more difficult it is to remain focused on a set of specific objectives.

In your quest to become a Demo Master, consider all of the people in your organization who interact with customers. Proactively build a relationship, a network, with those people who access and gather information that can be useful for you.

Exercise: Set up and execute a Demo Day. What did you learn?

Exercise: Make a list of all of the people in your organization who interact with your customers—organize this information as a table, with three columns. The first column is the name of the person. The second is the depart-

ment that person is in. In the third column, identify the type of information that person gathers or learns from your customers.

If you create this table in Word or Excel you'll be able to sort on the type of information you are interested in exploring.

Exercise: *Investigate and consider sponsoring the purchase and implementation of a knowledge management tool to support the pre-sales processes. You will typically want capabilities that enable the capture and sharing of best practices information, specific information on demos and tools, Situation Slides and Illustrations, and related resources.*

Current pre-sales folks will find this repository extremely useful in their day-to-day jobs. New hires will come up-to-speed much more rapidly that previously, due to easy access to the necessary information.

Two options to consider include DemoGurus (www.DemoGurus.com), a community web site, and StreetSmarts, by Involve Technology (www.InvolveTechnology.com).

Extend Thyself

As you become a Demo Master, you will find that you can both create and capitalize on opportunities. You can create opportunities in qualification meetings, as described above in Know Thy Competitors via diagnosing with a bias towards your capabilities or "adding rows". You can capitalize on opportunities as they arise in qualification meetings or in live demonstrations.

Here are some final ideas to help you extend yourself:

- Take and use customer examples whenever possible. This was introduced in the Technical Preparation chapter and is explored further in executing Tips and Tricks events. The ability to embrace and succeed with customer examples, particularly when they are offered on-the-fly is extremely powerful.

Accepting these challenges requires that you are very confident in your knowledge of your software and in your ability to translate your customers' problems into viable solutions on-the-fly. (Of course, isn't that what your software is supposed to offer, anyway?) Practicing and mastering skills associated with managing questions and To Do Lists are very important for your success with these examples.

Tips and Tricks sessions provide an excellent and relatively safe training ground for mastering tackling customer-proffered problems on-the-fly.

- Extend beyond the identified Specific Capabilities to show other capabilities that <u>become</u> relevant—through questions, additional qualification, etc.

- Extend by asking questions that would be addressed by other capabilities <u>you</u> have, to differentiate you from your competition, or to increase the perceived value of your Solution, or sell more of your product(s). One way to prepare for this is to perform "triage" on the overall list of capabilities that you can present in a demo, by categorizing capabilities as follows:

  - Specific Capabilities that are IN the demo. These you will have identified through qualification.

  - Capabilities that are NOT in the demo. These are capabilities that are clearly not relevant for the customer.

  - Capabilities that you hold in RESERVE. These are capabilities that <u>might</u> be important to the customer, that can differentiate you from competition or add additional perceived value to your Solution.

- Finally, one of the best ways to truly assimilate new information, new skills and new ideas, is to train someone else! The process of delivering training forces you to crystallize your understanding and clarify any points of confusion that you may have.

Exercise: Go and train someone else on the concepts and skills you've learned from this book and from practicing the ideas offered in this book.

Congratulations!

If you have applied the ideas in these chapters, and practiced, delivered, and refined your experiences, you may indeed become a Demo Master. There is no official diploma, however, and there is no clear definition of measuring your success. However, there are a number of critical factors that will tell you clearly that you have ascended to the exalted role of Demo Master.

As a Demo Master you should <u>expect</u> to be in demand. The sales force will specifically request your participation for key projects and critical meetings and demonstrations. Your customers will ask for your help in understanding and addressing new problems that they face. They will also ask for your help in introducing new users to your software. Third parties will know and respect you, and may ask for your participation in <u>their</u> users meetings.

While you will be in high demand, you also have an increased responsibility within your own organization (ask for a raise…). Your words will carry more weight in prioritizing new capabilities for development. Your customer support and consulting organizations may ask for your help in trouble-shooting problems at customer sites, and in promoting and delivering their services.

Finally, you have an additional responsibility—you must share your experiences and knowledge with newer hires. As a Demo Master, you must develop a training and skills development plan for the new SE's and other technical staff in your organization.

And that's a book in its own right…!

Glossary

Benefit:	The gain or advantage provided through the use of a Specific Capability by the customer.
Booth Shark:	A person staffing a booth at a trade show or conference charged with the responsibility of engaging and initially qualifying prospects.
Canned Demo:	A pre-prepared Generic Demo that is typically recorded for use when a human cannot deliver a live demo.
Capability:	A capability offered or available in a software package. A capability by itself is of little or no value.
CBI:	Critical Business Issue; the key problem that a customer must solve to achieve his or her major objectives.
Chain Of Pain:	The interrelationship between customer players' CBI's, Reasons and Specific Capabilities.
Champion:	A customer representative who willingly and actively supports the purchase and implementation of your capabilities. Champions will provide access to key people and other resources within a customer's organization.
Cosmetic Bug:	A bug that does not really impact the software's functionality, but rather impacts what is seen on the screen.
Database Breakeven Point:	The point in time where a database contains sufficient content to justify its use to a typical user.

Delta:	The difference between the customer's existing workflow or process, and the way the customer would like it to be.
Demo:	Short way of saying "Demonstration".
Demo Days:	Focused, mutual demonstration sessions put on by, and for the benefit of, the SE organization.
Demonstration:	The presentation of the set of Specific Capabilities needed to solve a customer's Critical Business Issue.
Direct Research:	The process of gathering information through direct contact with the customer.
Demonstration Roadmap:	A slide or set of slides that identifies the overall pathway and specific section for a complex demonstration involving multiple products or multiple Solutions.
"Do It"	The "Do It" is the most concise, rational pathway to proceed from the beginning of a demonstration to achieve the Illustration. It represents the fewest number of mouse clicks required to go from launching your software to generating that screen that is the Illustration.
"Do It Again"	The "Do It Again" is a second pass through the software, following the "Do It" pathway, but developing more details and providing richer explanation.
Earned Reputation:	The confluence of earned trust, demonstrated competence and efficacy, that a person achieves in the minds of customers.
Elevator Demo:	A concise, clear description of the solutions and applications that your product enables. The best Elevator Demos include providing one or more Illustrations as a take away piece.
Evaluation:	Hands-on technical proof, by a customer.
Feature:	A capability offered or available in a software package. A feature by itself is of little or no value.
Generic Demo:	A demonstration given to an unqualified audience.

Good Question:	A question asked by the audience during a demonstration that is meaningful.
Great Demo!:	The managed, effective process of presenting the Specific Capabilities needed by a customer.
Great Question:	A question asked by the audience during a demo that supports or reinforces the value of a Specific Capability, or a question asked by the audience that assists the flow of the demonstration.
Illustration:	A concise, visual method of communicating the reality, or proof, of a Solution.
Indirect Research:	The process of gathering information through indirect channels, without direct contact with the customer. Indirect Research can include papers, publications, web sites, patents, product documentation, etc.
Infrastructure Checklist:	The list of all hardware, software, network, audio-visual, facilities and other requirements needed for a demonstration.
Interdependency:	The linkage between people or events, wherein one or more people's actions or events will positively or negatively impact others in the same organization.
Introduction:	For a demo, the Introduction provides the audience with the outline of the demo. It is the demonstration agenda
Not Now List:	A method of queuing and organizing a list of questions and issues from an audience during the course of a demo. The Not Now List provides the demonstrator with the ability to manage and control questions, answers, the pace of the demo and the audience.
Outline:	An Outline defines the presence and order for the building blocks of a demo. It can also provide the basic text for your Introduction.
Project:	A specific sales process, often called a "deal". "Project" is more accurate, and realistic, as a Project entails the definition of players, project management parameters, a beginning, and an end.

Qualification:	The process of identifying the Critical Business Issues, Reasons, and Specific Capabilities needed for a particular customer.
Reason:	The sub-problems that individually or collectively are responsible for the customer's inability to solve their Critical Business Issue.
Recorded Demo:	A pre-prepared Generic Demo that is typically recorded for use when a human cannot deliver a live demo.
Remote Demo:	Demonstrations where the audience is physically separated from the presenter.
Reference Story:	A Situation Slide used to generate "hope and curiosity" in Vision Generation demos and Qualification meetings.
Rollover Agreement:	A license agreement for an evaluation that presupposes a successful completion and streamlines the legal process.
Sales Methodology:	A process or method of managing and executing sales. Popular methods include "CustomerCentric Selling", "Solution Selling", VITO, SPIN, Miller-Heiman, and others.
Salesperson:	The person in the Selling Team responsible for identify a customer's Critical Business Issues, Reasons, and Specific Capabilities, and for organizing the method, objectives and timing for delivering technical proof via a Great Demo!
SE:	A "Sales Engineer"—a technical resource expected to be fluent in the capabilities and operating environments of a company's products.
Selling Team:	Typically a Selling Team, or Sales Team, consists of a Salesperson and a SE. More complex compositions may be expected for more complex sales situations. For example, a Consultant may be included in the Selling Team if product customization is planned or needed, as part of the Project.
Serious Bug:	A bug that impacts software functionality so as to make it unusable.

Sequence of Events:	A tool used for Evaluations and other sales processes that organizes and orchestrates the players, tasks, timing and responsibilities.
Situation Slide:	Presented immediately prior to showing an Illustration, the Situation Slide for Technical Proof demos recalls Company, Job Title, CBI, Reason, Specific Capabilities and Delta information previously uncovered in Qualification. For Vision Generation Demos, a Situation Slide may be a Reference Story.
Solution:	The set of Specific Capabilities provided by your company, in context, that solves a customer's Critical Business Issue. A Solution can come from capabilities in a single product or service, or across several products or services, or a combination of products and services.
Specific Capability:	A capability that is required to address or solve a customer's Critical Business Issue.
Situation Slide:	A slide, often created using PowerPoint, that includes Situation information (job title, company, industry, CBI, Reasons, Specific Capabilities and the Delta) and used as an integral part of presenting Illustrations.
Stupid Question:	A question asked by the audience during a demonstration that is not meaningful.
Tips and Tricks Session:	A problem-solving and "how to" session held at a customer site.
To Do List:	A method of queuing and organizing a list of capabilities and Specific Capabilities desired by an audience. Typically this method is used "on the fly", for identifying and listing audience needs, Critical Business Issues, Reasons, and especially Specific Capabilities.
Workflow:	A series of interdependent steps or sub-processes executed by members of a customer's organization to achieve a specific outcome.

Appendixes

1. Meeting Information Sheet—Example

2. Meeting Information Sheet—Blank

3. Demonstration Information Sheet—Example

4. Demonstration Information Sheet—Blank

5. Infrastructure Checklist

6. Customer Meeting Preparation Sheet—Example

7. Sequence Of Events—Example

8. Example Illustrations and Menu in MS Publisher

9. Example Great Demo! Using Microsoft Word

10. Reading List

Meeting Information Sheet—Example

Meeting Location: ABC Software Corporation
333 3rd Avenue
Centerville, AZ 12345

Meeting Date: Monday October 24, 2005.

Meeting Start Time: 9:00 AM

Meeting Ends: 10:30 AM

Meeting Objective: Technical Proof—Demonstrate Specific Capabilities agreed upon as a Solution

Specific Roles/Timing:

9:00 AM	Introduction—Steve Maybill
9:10 AM	Review of Objectives, Reasons, and Specific Capabilities to Demonstrated—Salesperson
9:30 AM	Demonstration—SE
10:00 AM	Q & A—SE
10:10 AM	Summary—SE
10:20 AM	Next Steps and Wrap-Up—Salesperson
10:30 AM	Meeting Concludes

Customer Contact:

Steve Maybill, VP Sales

Telephone: +1 (555) 555 1212

Email: Smaybill@ABCSoftCorp.com

Other Notes: Meet Steve Maybill in Lobby of Building 1 at 8:50 AM

Meeting Information Sheet—Blank

Meeting Location:

Meeting Date:

Meeting Start Time:

Meeting Ends:

Meeting Objective:

Specific Roles/Timing:

Customer Contact:

Other Notes:

[Feel free to copy this form for your own use. You may also want to consider ensuring that the information in this form can be captured in your organization's CRM or SFA system]

Demonstration Information Sheet—Example

Customer: ABC Software, Inc.

Meeting
Date: October 24, 2005 at 9:00 AM

Customer Organization Charts and Chain(s) of Pain:

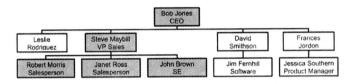

Meeting   Technical Proof.
Objective:

Customer CBI's, Reasons, and Specific Capabilities:

CEO:

  CBI: Unable to increase shareholder value sufficiently, as measured
              by the stock price, on a quarter-by-quarter basis.

  Reason: Quarterly revenues, and hence profits, are less than expected
              by analysts.

VP Sales:

  CBI: Unable to achieve quarterly corporate revenue targets with
              existing product lines and sales staff.

  Reason: Salespeople, as a whole, are not achieving quarterly quotas.

Salesperson:

  CBI: Unable to achieve quarterly quotas on a regular basis.

  Reason: Product demonstrations fail to close the technical sale.

Specific Capabilities Needed:

  1. Great Demo! skills and methods for the SE in the Project.

  2. Elucidation and communication, to the SE, of the CBI's,
  Reasons, and Specific capabilities of the customer.

SE:

CBI: Unable to produce demonstrations sufficient to close the technical sale in the time-frame required.

Reason: Lack of demonstration skills and understanding of customer CBI's and Reasons.

Specific Capabilities Needed:

1. Great Demo! skills and methods.

2. Clear communication of the Specific Capabilities needed to be demonstrated in the upcoming Demo.

Meeting Information Sheet: (Attached)

Demonstration Information Sheet—Blank

Customer:

Meeting Date:

Customer Organization Charts and Chain(s) of Pain:

Meeting Objective:

Customer CBI's, Reasons, and Specific Capabilities:

Meeting Information Sheet: (Attached)

[Feel free to copy this form for your own use. You may also want to consider ensuring that the information in this form can be captured in your organization's CRM or SFA system]

Infrastructure Checklist—Example

Item	Confirmed	Quantity
Hardware:		
Laptop Computer OK:	☐ Yes ☐ No	
• Sufficient space on hard disk.	☐ Yes ☐ No	
• RAM sufficient for application.	☐ Yes ☐ No	
• Modem operating correctly.	☐ Yes ☐ No	
• Screen resolution OK.	☐ Yes ☐ No	
Network or Server Computer OK:	☐ Yes ☐ No	
• Sufficient space on hard disk.	☐ Yes ☐ No	
• RAM sufficient for application.	☐ Yes ☐ No	
• Modem operating correctly.	☐ Yes ☐ No	
• Network connections OK.	☐ Yes ☐ No	
Modem Connections:	☐ Yes ☐ No	
• Telephone cabling OK.	☐ Yes ☐ No	
• Telephone line OK.	☐ Yes ☐ No	
• Dialing requirements clear.	☐ Yes ☐ No	
Network Connections OK:	☐ Yes ☐ No	
• Network cabling OK.	☐ Yes ☐ No	
• Network connections available.	☐ Yes ☐ No	
• Network operating OK.	☐ Yes ☐ No	

Item	Confirmed	Quantity
• Connection requirements clear.	□ Yes □ No	
Other Computer Equipment?	□ Yes □ No	
•	□ Yes □ No	
•		
•	□ Yes □ No	
•		
•	□ Yes □ No	
•		
Projection OK:	□ Yes □ No	
• Computer compatibility OK.	□ Yes □ No	
• Screen resolution OK.	□ Yes □ No	
• Projector availability OK.	□ Yes □ No	
• Operation clear.	□ Yes □ No	
Other Projection Equipment:		
• Overhead Projector.	□ Yes □ No	
• RF Mouse.	□ Yes □ No	
• Laser Pointer.	□ Yes □ No	
• Videotape, VCR, TV Monitor.	□ Yes □ No	
• CD-ROM drive.	□ Yes □ No	

Item	Confirmed	Quantity

Power:

- Voltage/Current/Adapters OK.   □ Yes □ No
- Plugs OK.   □ Yes □ No
- Extension Cord(s) OK.   □ Yes □ No
- Power Strip(s) OK.   □ Yes □ No

Lighting:

- Dimming/darkening OK.   □ Yes □ No
- Lights operation clear.   □ Yes □ No

Screen(s):

- Projection screen(s) OK.   □ Yes □ No
- Projection screen(s) available.   □ Yes □ No
- Screen size OK.   □ Yes □ No
- Screen operation clear.   □ Yes □ No

Audio:

- Microphone required?   □ Yes □ No
- Microphone available.   □ Yes □ No
- Microphone operation clear.   □ Yes □ No

Whiteboard or Flipchart:

- Whiteboards needed?   □ Yes □ No
- Whiteboards confirmed.   □ Yes □ No

Item	Confirmed	Quantity
• Flipcharts needed?	□ Yes □ No	
• Flipcharts confirmed?	□ Yes □ No	
Other Presentation Equipment?	□ Yes □ No	
•	□ Yes □ No	
Handouts:		
• Illustration (s) copies.	□ Yes □ No	
• Brochures.	□ Yes □ No	
• Fact Sheets.	□ Yes □ No	
• White Papers.	□ Yes □ No	
• Reference Stories.	□ Yes □ No	
• Corporate Folders.	□ Yes □ No	
• Corporate Backgrounders.	□ Yes □ No	
•	□ Yes □ No	
•	□ Yes □ No	
•	□ Yes □ No	
•	□ Yes □ No	
Software:		
Laptop Computer Software OK:	□ Yes □ No	
• Operating system OK.	□ Yes □ No	
• MS Office OK.	□ Yes □ No	
• Product software OK.	□ Yes □ No	
• Ancillary products OK.	□ Yes □ No	

Item	Confirmed	Quantity
Network/Server Software OK:	☐ Yes ☐ No	
• Server software OK.	☐ Yes ☐ No	
• Network software OK.	☐ Yes ☐ No	
• Web server OK.	☐ Yes ☐ No	
• Database software OK.	☐ Yes ☐ No	
• Database demo tables OK.	☐ Yes ☐ No	

Customer Meeting Preparation Sheet—Example

Item	Responsibility	Confirmed
Travel:		☐ Yes ☐ No
• Flight Arrangements.	Customer	☐ Yes ☐ No
• Hotel reservations.	Assistant	☐ Yes ☐ No
• Local transport.	Assistant	☐ Yes ☐ No
• Local transport Info:		
• Dinner reservations.	Assistant	☐ Yes ☐ No
• Dinner Info:		
• Assistant's Contact Info:		
Meeting Infrastructure:		☐ Yes ☐ No
• Meeting room reserved.	Assistant	☐ Yes ☐ No
• Tables/chairs organized.	Assistant	☐ Yes ☐ No
• Computer screens clean.	Assistant	☐ Yes ☐ No
• Cabling orderly and safe.	Assistant	☐ Yes ☐ No
• Debris removed.	Assistant	☐ Yes ☐ No
• Whiteboards clean.	Assistant	☐ Yes ☐ No
• Refreshments organized.	Assistant	☐ Yes ☐ No
• Literature prepared.	Assistant	☐ Yes ☐ No
• Literature:		
• Giveaways ready.	Assistant	☐ Yes ☐ No
• Giveaways:		

[Feel free to copy this form for your own use. You may also want to consider ensuring that the information in this form can be captured in your organization's CRM or SFA system]

Example Sequence of Events

Event	Track	Comments	Target Start Date	Target Complete Date	Complete
Get agreement from Management to proceed.	Financial/ Licensing/ Admin.			7/9/04	√
Identify Champion(s) for Project at Customer.		Steve Maybill, Jessica Southern	7/9/04	7/9/04	√
Meeting to Develop Project Plan & Business Case.	Technical			7/17/04	
Deliver Project Proposal Draft to Customer.	Financial/ Licensing/ Admin.		7/9/04	7/20/04	
Draft Agreement written, delivered to Customer Legal.	Legal		7/9/04	7/23/04	
Customer IT Infrastructure Assessment.	Technical	Oracle installation.	7/14/04	7/21/04	
Negotiation of Agreement.	Legal		7/23/04	7/26/04	
Capital spending approval.	Financial/ Licensing/ Admin.			8/2/04	

Event	Track	Comments	Target Start Date	Target Complete Date	Complete
Final Agreement approved.	Legal			8/2/04	
Customer IT infrastructure ready (Go/No Go).	Financial/ Licensing/ Admin.		7/21/04	8/2/04	
Final sign-off of Agreement.	Financial/ Licensing			8/2/04	
Installation and Administrator Training at Customer.	Technical		8/12/04	8/13/04	
Complete Installation Acceptance Tests.	Technical	Confirm operation and performance	8/14/04	8/14/04	
End-user training at Customer.	Technical	16 users; two ½-day sessions.	8/17/04	8/18/04	
Begin running Customer Projects.	Technical	See Project definitions.	8/19/04	8/27/04	
End of Evaluation Period.	Technical			8/30/04	
Data analysis and decision meeting. (Go/ no go).	Technical		8/30/04	9/9/04	
Automatic Roll-over deadline.	Financial/ Licensing			9/10/04	

Event	Track	Comments	Target Start Date	Target Complete Date	Complete
Installation/ preparation for initial deployment.	Technical		9/14/04	9/15/04	
Training for initial deployment.	Technical		9/21/04	9/22/04	
ROI progress review meeting.	Financial/ Licensing/ Admin.		11/9/04		

[Feel free to copy this form for your own use. You may also want to consider ensuring that the information in this form can be captured in your organization's CRM or SFA system]

Example Illustrations and Menu Approach in Microsoft Publisher

Microsoft Publisher does a terrific job in providing sets of Illustrations targeted for various customers and potential uses. Furthermore, the way that these Illustrations are presented is an excellent example of a Menu approach for Generic Demos.

When you first start Publisher, you are presented with a list of "Designs" organized by category:

- Quick Publications
- Word Documents
- Newsletters
- Websites
- Brochures
- Catalogs
- Flyers
- Signs
- Postcards
- Invitation Cards
- Greeting Cards
- Business Cards
- Resumes
- Letterheads
- Envelopes
- Etc.

To the right of this list are thumbnails of the actual example publications, showing you what your publication will look like when completed (as a template). This is a very efficient and effective approach to addressing a broad range of potential users, needs, and situations.

The template Illustrations are wonderful, because the user is presented with an example of a completed publication for each template. Users can quickly see what their publication will look like—and they can very rapidly choose whether that specific template is what they want to use.

The Menu presentation is very well executed, since it is task-based and does not need to pre-suppose anything other than an example of the desired output. Further, the hierarchical organization of the Menu of templates enables users to "drill-down" to explore further or narrow their choices.

Finally, this presentation of template Illustrations is a terrific example for Generic Demo situations. Users select the output (task) they are interested in; the software then guides the user through a wizard to create a customized publication. (That is, by the way, a great example of a "Do It" pathway!)

If you are contemplating creating Generic or Menu-based Demos for an upcoming trade-show, or for your web-site, or CD-ROM or similar vehicle, invest a few minutes to explore how Publisher's example might apply to creating a series of demos for your own software.

Note: If you do not have Publisher on your machine, you can at least access some of Microsoft's templates at http://office.microsoft.com/en-us/templates/default.aspx.

Example Great Demo! For Microsoft Word

Imagine that you are a customer, the date is 1988 and that you are just being exposed to the "new" generation of word processors. You have a broad range of products to choose from, including WordPerfect, Microsoft Word, AmiPro, WordStar, WordMaster and others.

You decide that the new word processors may offer a solution to your business problem: you need to create business letters of one or two pages that include your company's logo on page one and an appropriate header on the second page. You need to bring a higher level of efficiency to your office and typing letters manually is taking too much time and staff. You ask for a demonstration of each of the packages above from their vendors.

Now think about the myriad of features and capabilities in Microsoft Word—as of 2004, there were well over 300 top-level menu choices and tools presented to users in the standard Word implementation (holy cow!). Imagine how long it might take to demonstrate all of the capabilities represented…

If you were to prepare a demonstration for yourself, as a customer, what would you include in the demo?

Here's a simple scenario for Word that helps to illustrate, well, Illustrations—and the "Do It" and "Do It Again" pathways.

The Illustrations

The best Illustration(s) for the scenario above are a one or more completed business letters:

Illustration Number 1: A completed business letter one page in length, including the company's logo at the top (for example), address, date and salutation, text, and signature line.

Illustration Number 2: A completed business letter two pages in length, the same as in Illustration Number 1, but with a suitable header at the top of page 2.

In your demo, you would present the first Illustration, describe what the customer is seeing, and then note the comparison between they way the customer created the business letter before (laboriously typed, with numerous "white-out" corrections, on an IBM Selectric type-writer) and they way it was done using your word processor (type the text, page in the logo graphic, and print—wow!).

You would then present the second Illustration, highlighting the addition of page 2 with the header. Again, you would compare this with how that same letter had been created before.

At this point the customer would say, "How did you create those letters?"

Do It

Your response is the "Do It" segment.

Your "Do It" would start with a blank document in your word processor, into which you'd paste the business text. You'd add the address, date, salutation and signature line. You would then paste in the logo graphic and finish by showing the final document (Illustration Number 1) in "Print Preview".

You'd then summarize what you had just completed.

Do It Again

A simple "Do It Again" would follow the same pathway as the Do It segment, however, you would paste in additional text to span two pages. You would then show inserting and completing a header. As with the "Do It", you would finish by showing the completed two-page document (Illustration Number 2) in "Print Preview".

Again, you'd summarize what you'd shown.

Note that in real-life, in this scenario, a customer might begin to ask questions of logical follow-on capabilities. One might expect them to ask, for example:

"Can I change the font and font size?"

"Can I change the formatting of the text?"

"Is there an automated way to input the date or other repetitious information?"

These questions can become a basis for your next "Do It Again" segment for your next customer.

That's a very simple example of a Great Demo!

What You Didn't Show...

Think again about the incredible range of features, commands, options and capabilities available in Microsoft Word. It would take all year (or more!) to show all of these.

For the demo above you wouldn't show how to do a table of contents or an index. Why? Because those capabilities aren't relevant for a one—or two-page business letter.

Conversely, if you were presenting Word to someone who wanted to create a book, then it might be very relevant to include table of contents creation, indexing, style sheets, and other functions relevant to writing a book.

In Summary

Identify, through qualification or discovery, the deliverables (as Illustrations) and the <u>Specific Capabilities</u> needed by the customer. Present those Illustrations to show proof or to generate a vision of a solution, following by the Specific Capabilities needed to create those Illustrations.

Reading List

The following books are recommended reading for your edification and amusement. Each offers a set of excellent information or provides skills that support and complement the material in this book. Retail prices are based on undiscounted prices online with Barnes and Noble (www.barnesandnoble.com) or Amazon (www.amazon.com). Check with the online stores for the most current prices.

"Crossing The Chasm: Marketing and Selling High-Tech Products to Mainstream Customers"

Author(s): Geoffrey Moore

HarperBusiness (HarperCollins Publishers, Incorporated), Paperback, 256pp. August 2002 (revised).

ISBN: 0060517123

Retail Price: $17.95

Notes: This is the book that changed many sales and marketing people's thinking about how to understand customers and sell software. Understanding the technology adoption curve and associated "chasm" can be critical in creating and delivering targeted demonstrations. Awareness of the type of customer (e.g., early adopter, early majority, etc.) can have enormous impact on what to include in a demonstration and how to present it. This book is highly recommended!

(More recent information may be found on the DemoGurus Community Website at www.DemoGurus.com).

"CustomerCentric Selling"

Author(s): Michael Bosworth and John Holland

McGraw-Hill Trade, Hardback, 304pp. November 2003.

ISBN: 0071425454

Retail Price: $29.95

Notes: Michael Bosworth was the author of the original "Solution Selling" sales methodology, which is one of the most popular methods in use today. CustomerCentric Selling is the evolutionary replacement for "Solution Selling" and offers a more direct approach to consultative sales. In particular, the concept of searching for a customer's "pain" is replaced with a quest to understand and sell to a customer's objectives.

(More recent information may be found on the DemoGurus Community Website at www.DemoGurus.com).

"Making the Technical Sale: Real-World Training for the Successful Sales Consultant"

Author(s): James F. Milbery and Richard E. Greenwald

Muska & Lipmann Publishing, Paperback, 400pp. March 2001.

ISBN: 0966288998

Retail Price: $34.95

Notes: An excellent text for Sales Engineers, Product Managers, and related job titles. This book provides a good roadmap to help understand the key aspects of the technical sales process. A chapter on demonstrations offers some basics to help get organized for a new practitioner.

(More recent information may be found on the DemoGurus Community Website at www.DemoGurus.com).

"Solution Selling: Creating Buyers In Difficult Selling Markets"

Author(s): Michael Bosworth

McGraw-Hill Trade, Hardback, 224pp. September 1994.

ISBN: 0786303158

Retail Price: $29.95

Notes: This is the original "Solution Selling" sales methodology book, from which a substantial amount of "controlled vocabulary" terms have been utilized for this book, including, for example, "Critical Business Issue"). Solution Selling, as a methodology, was one of the first and most successful consultative selling methods. If you have the time, it may be worthwhile to read "Solution Selling" first, followed by "CustomerCentric Selling". If you feel you only have time for one such book, start with "CustomerCentric Selling".

(More recent information may be found on the DemoGurus Community Website at www.DemoGurus.com).

"Permission Marketing: Turning Strangers Into Friends and Friends Into Customers"

Author(s): Seth Godin

Simon & Schuster, Hardback, 256pp. May 1999.

ISBN: 0684856360

Retail Price: $25.00

Notes: It is estimated that every day we are subjected to ~3,000 "interruption"-based marketing messages—on TV, the internet, magazines, radio, billboards, newspapers, etc. [Must be true: I counted 120 display advertisements in a typical morning edition of my local newspaper in the sections I normally peruse—this doesn't include the classified or the additional "advertising package".] Permission marketing seeks to engage customers in a more comfortable, step-wise process and develop a relationship over time. "Opt-In" options for email newsletters are an example of this process. This book is an excellent source to gain an introduction to permission-based marketing approaches—and to challenge your thinking if you are operating with a traditional "interruption"-based marketing strategy today.

(More recent information may be found on the DemoGurus Community Website at www.DemoGurus.com).

"The 7 Habits of Highly Effective People: Powerful Lessons in Personal Change"

Author(s): Stephen R. Covey

Free Press, Paperback, 358pp. September 1990.

ISBN: 0671708635

Retail Price: $15.00

Notes: After approximately 15 years in print, this book still has an "Amazon.com Sales Ranking" of <100—which means that it is still being purchased in high volume. There are excellent ideas and concepts to be gleaned and practiced in this book. It makes excellent reading on a few cross-country flights, as you need some time to reflect on what you have absorbed and decide whether and/or how to apply the ideas. Some of the strongest lessons include balancing execution with preparation—the "Sharpen the Saw" concepts—which are also founding principles of the Great Demo! method.

(More recent information may be found on the DemoGurus Community Website at www.DemoGurus.com).

"The Tipping Point: How Little Things Can Make a Big Difference"

Author(s): Malcolm Gladwell

Back Bay Books, Paperback, 304pp. January 2002.

ISBN: 0316346624

Retail Price: $14.95

Notes: While Gladwell doesn't offer a process or toolkit to harness word-of-mouth effects, he is one of the first (and most readable) authors to identify and frame a useful vocabulary around word-of-mouth. Terms such as "mavens", "connectors", and "salesmen" describe three key personalities that serve as the power, amplifiers, and circuitry for word-of-mouth. The Tipping Point draws a more direct analogy from the world of biology: word-of-mouth effects and the results of these effects are likened to viruses and epidemics. In fact, Gladwell uses epidemics as examples to explore and understand how they relate to word-of-mouth. This is an excellent book to provide the reader with a good basis for understanding the overall concepts of word-of-mouth. See also "Unleashing the Ideavirus" for interesting examples of word-of-mouth effects in the world of marketing.

(More recent information may be found on the DemoGurus Community Website at www.DemoGurus.com).

"Unleashing the Ideavirus"

Author(s): Seth Godin, Malcolm Gladwell

Hyperion, Hardback, 234pp. October 2001.

ISBN: 0786887176

Retail Price: $14.00

Notes: Word-of-mouth is one of the most effective, and certainly powerful, marketing methods. Word-of-mouth opinions can make or break a product or a company, regardless of the use and extent of other "traditional" channels (e.g., advertising). Are there methods and practices that can be used to identify and harness word-of-mouth? The concept of the "ideavirus" embodies both word-of-mouth marketing concepts, and product design and implementation ideas that can cause people to spread products like, well, viruses! This book is one of a series of Seth Godin's efforts that build upon one another, in general, and on Gladwell's "The Tipping Point", specifically. Notwithstanding, you can read it by itself and take away a great deal that may be readily and directly applicable on a day-to-day basis. It certainly will stimulate novel and interesting thinking!

(More recent information may be found on the DemoGurus Community Website at www.DemoGurus.com).

Title: "The Anatomy of Buzz"

Author(s): Emanuel Rosen

Currency, Paperback, 303pp. April 2002.

ISBN: 0385496680

Retail Price: $14.95

Notes: Gladwell's "The Tipping Point" draws our attention to the idea of "word-of-mouth"; Seth Godin shows us <u>what</u> kinds of remarkable things can be achieved using viral marketing techniques; Emanuel Rosen's "The Anatomy of Buzz" walks us through <u>how</u> to make word-of-mouth marketing work for our own businesses. This is an <u>excellent</u> book! It lays out a pathway to follow and provides pragmatic guidelines and best practices, verbally illustrated using real-world examples. A business book is a success for me if I find I've made a few notes while reading the book (and acted on those notes). In reading "The Anatomy of Buzz" I generated <u>dozens</u> of notes and ideas—many of which have been implemented or are in process today. This is an <u>excellent</u> book. I'll say it again: This is an <u>excellent</u> book! I strongly recommend it to those who have "marketing", business development", "sales", or "founder" in their job titles.

(More recent information may be found on the DemoGurus Community Website at <u>www.DemoGurus.com</u>).

About the Author

Peter Cohan founded The Second Derivative in 2003 to help organizations increase the probability of success in their sales and marketing processes. The Second Derivative provides a range of workshops, coaching, consulting, and skills development capabilities, with a particular focus on the needs of organizations developing and selling software.

In July 2004, he launched and began moderating DemoGurus™, a community web exchange that provides ongoing guidance and information sharing for people who create and deliver software demonstrations.

Peter has authored numerous papers and presentations, and has a successful track-record as a presenter at trade conferences and seminars. Most recently, he wrote and published this second edition to "Great Demo!" to continue to update, practice, and communicate the Great Demo! methodology for creating and delivering novel, compelling demonstrations.

Prior to The Second Derivative, Peter enjoyed over 20 years in software—in senior management, business development, sales and marketing roles. In 1998, he joined Symyx Technologies, Inc. to found Symyx' Discovery Tools® business, which focused on levering Symyx' developed technology through providing access to systems, software, and intellectual property. As Vice President Discovery Tools, and thereafter President Symyx Discovery Tools, Inc. (wholly owned by Symyx Technologies, Inc.) Mr. Cohan grew the organization from an empty spreadsheet into a $30MM per year business. As of this writing it represents one of Symyx' major business legs, providing fully integrated workflows to customers in pharmaceutical and chemical research.

Prior to Symyx, he was Vice President Customer Marketing at MDL Information Systems, Inc. In 13.5 years at MDL, Peter gained experience in the creation, sales, implementation, and deployment of software tools and systems in support of pharmaceutical, agrochemical, and chemical research. His roles at MDL ran from Technical Marketing, to Product Marketing and Management, Field Marketing, Sales and Sales Management, and finally Marketing Management. In 1993-1995, he was posted to MDL's European Headquarters, located in Allschwil, Switzerland, to drive the deployment of their flagship offering into their key European customers.

Previously, he held various research and technical positions at Calbiochem-Behring Corporation, including working in Immunochemistry R&D, Clinical Chemistry R&D and Product Technical Support—during which time it is believed he was the first person to successfully freeze-dry beer. He has a degree in Chemistry from the University of California at San Diego.

A key driving force in founding The Second Derivative was (and continues to be) Peter's wife, Diane, and their two curiously-above-average children, Kelsey and Mackenzie.

He has been, and continues to be, a customer.

Index

0-595-34559-X